AGAINST
ALL
ODDS

*From Surviving to Thriving with
My Unbeatable God*

Pastor Stephen M. Colbert Sr.

WESTBOW
PRESS®
A DIVISION OF THOMAS NELSON
& ZONDERVAN

Scripture taken from the King James Version of the Bible.

Scripture quotations marked (NIV) are taken from the Holy Bible, New International Version®, NIV®. Copyright © 1973, 1978, 1984, 2011 by Biblica, Inc.™ Used by permission of Zondervan. All rights reserved worldwide. www.zondervan.com The "NIV" and "New International Version" are trademarks registered in the United States Patent and Trademark Office by Biblica, Inc.

WestBow Press books may be ordered through booksellers or by contacting:

WestBow Press
A Division of Thomas Nelson & Zondervan
1663 Liberty Drive
Bloomington, IN 47403
www.westbowpress.com
1 (866) 928-1240

Because of the dynamic nature of the Internet, any web addresses or links contained in this book may have changed since publication and may no longer be valid. The views expressed in this work are solely those of the author and do not necessarily reflect the views of the publisher, and the publisher hereby disclaims any responsibility for them.

Any people depicted in stock imagery provided by Thinkstock are models, and such images are being used for illustrative purposes only. Certain stock imagery © Thinkstock.

ISBN: 978-1-9736-1501-9 (sc)
ISBN: 978-1-9736-1500-2 (e)

Print information available on the last page.

WestBow Press rev. date: 03/21/2018

In Memory of

My Mom, Anna Geraldine Torian, My Sister, Corinthia Ann Tate, My Brother, Wilbur Torian, My Aunt, Inez Scovens, My Aunt, Claudette Bradley, My Uncle Lawrence Colbert, My Grand-Father, Bernard Colbert Sr., and My Grand-Mother, Julia Colbert

Dedication

I dedicate this book to Mrs. Lisa d. Tisdale, a phenomenal woman of God who has demonstrated rare and unusual faith and endurance in the midst of a persistent medical condition. Lisa, you are my Shero! – On November 12, 2017 the City of Hope Church instituted the "Lisa Darnell H.O.P.E. AWARD" in recognition of her faithful and inspirational acts towards **H**elping **O**ther **P**eople through **E**mpowerment. Well done Lisa!

The book is also dedicated to anyone who may be struggling to overcome A traumatic experience or condition in their lives. I believe that with God's help, ordinary people can survive and thrive against all odds. This book is also dedicated to those individuals who have survived life threatening medical conditions or mental disorders and are currently thriving in life. No weapon formed against you will prosper!

Contents

Special Thanks

I thank God for the plan he designed for my life before I was conceived in my mother's womb. I thank my Lord and Savior, Jesus Christ who is God revealed in human flesh. I will be forever grateful for the personal relationship I have experienced with Jesus Christ for the past 32 years of my life. I thank the Lord for being so faithful to me throughout this process and throughout my life.

To my wonderful wife, who next to God, is the only person in my life who knows and loves every inch of my being. She is my biggest supporter and encourager. Thank you for being so patient for so long. I love you so much Baby.

To my two precious children, Stacie Nicole and Stephen Jr., who inspire me every day and believe in me and the ministry God has called me to do. You are a part of my purpose in life. You are so intertwined in my daily life and thoughts to the extent that I never go a day without you on my mind. I love you guys more than you will ever know. I pray that each of you will fulfill your destiny and be all that God created you to be.

To my sister, Joanna, who I watched survive and thrive beyond her addiction to alcohol. She inspired me and encouraged me so greatly in and through all of my medical challenges. I am in my right mind today because of how I watched God keep you together through your darkest days. Now you are a bright light for so many people who were helped by your life and testimony. I love you Joanna.

To my sister, Sheila, who I also watched survive and thrive beyond substance abuse, incarceration and homelessness. This sister was a surrogate mother to me through high school and college. She never hesitated to provide those things I needed that my mother was not able to give me. I must admit that She favored me over the other siblings. She saw a success in my future, even when I did not have a clue. I love you Sheila!

To my youngest sister, Almeta, who I also watched go through what I considered the most traumatic experiences a young girl could ever imagine. You helped me to believe that nothing is too hard for God.

I watched God sustain you through some things that most people would have not have survived. You refused to quit, even when it seemed like everything and every person in your life had forsaken you. You are a miracle girl. I watched you endure pain for so long and now you are enjoying the best days of your life. Thank you for hanging in life against all odds.

To my best friend since the age of eight-teen, Fred Wright, thank you for sticking with over the long haul. We were once partners in crime but now we are partners in Christ. Thank you for providing me with helpful feedback about the book in it's early stages. I believe you have enough experience with God to write your own book some day.

To one of my best friends in ministry, Rev. Terry Thornton, Pastor of the Sweet Hope Freewill Baptist Church, Baltimore Md. Terry, you are much younger than me in age, but you are one of the most humble and wisest men I have ever known. We started out in ministry together in 1989. I have always been able to lean on you for support and words of encouragement.

I have watched you, your beautiful wife, Jacqueline, your two sons, Terry II and Benjamin grow together as a family in Christ. I thank you for trusting me to preach to your congregation each August and being blessed by your friendship and fellowship. I look forward to sharing with you as we journey with Jesus in ministry. Thank you for being transparent and down to earth.

You always present the best version of yourself where ever I see you. Thanks buddy!

To my Bishop, Rev. Walter S. Thomas, Pastor of the New Psalmist Baptist Church, Baltimore Md. Thank you Bishop Thomas for believing in me and encouraging me from the time I informed you of my calling to preach the Gospel and from the time that I shared the vision God gave me to organize the City of Hope Church. Between those two milestones you were always there for me and my family at critical times in our lives. You are the greatest male role model I know. I learned so much from you about life, marriage, fatherhood and ministry. I even tried whistling like you, but you are the only one who has ability to whistle while you preach. I strive to make the City of Hope Church the kind of ministry that reflects the love, compassion, and faithfulness that you have demonstrated to New Psalmist and the world. You have influenced a countless number of people to accept Jesus Christ as their personal Lord and Savior. You are one of God's most humble and graceful human beings on the planet and I'm so grateful that I had a chance to be pastored by you. Thank you Bishop! Thank you 1st Lady Patricia Thomas, for sharing your husband with thousands of people over the years and the thousands yet to come.

To my entire extended family and all my friends, thank you and I love you all. I want to especially thank my Aunt Dorothy Robinson, for showing our family a model of prayer, faith, strength and womanhood in the face of adversity. To my

Aunt Concetta Colbert, thank you for caring for me upon my discharge from the hospital after the near fatal car accident. When I was eight years young, you nursed me back to good health and strength on the couch at 620 St. Ann's Ave. Thank you Aunt Dottie for being Eighty-Six Strong.

To my City of Hope Church Family, thank you for your prayers and support. Thank you for embracing me and my family in love. Thank you for allowing me to be your first Pastor. Thank you for making our Church a place — "Where Hope Is Contagious!

To my Barber, Mitch Mitchell, thank you for listening to my stories as you cut my hair. I have hope that my experiences helped you in some way. I will always remember the wisdom filled conversations we had at Celebrity Cuts Barber Shop and how they inspired me to write my story in this book. Thank you ladies and gentlemen for providing an environment that allowed everyone to express their opinions without being judged.

To Ms. Fannie Hughes, my personal Notary Public Agent. Thank you for Providing your service for the book permission statements. I will never forget your smile and the encouragement you expressed each time I asked you to notarize a book permission statement. A BIG KUDOS TO YOU!

To Pastor Reginald Lawrence, thank you for being a mentor and role model for me in the Baltimore City Public School Central Office and in Ministry. Thank you for being my Barnabas and my Silas at the same time.

To Mrs. Karen (Leading Lady) Lawrence, for your friendship, counsel, and prayers as my co-worker in the fire-pot of Baltimore City Public School Leadership. You were one of the three principals that I trusted to teach me how to lead. Thank you for being my B.E.O.-"Book Editing Officer".

To my Mother, who is present with the Lord, for being the greatest person in my world. Mom, you cherished me, you nurtured me and you always believed in me, even though I disappointed you so many times.

You were there for me, my brother and my sisters through the good times and the bad times. You sacrificed so much for us. You taught your children how to survive by allowing us to watch you survive through some of the most devastating experiences in your life. We watched you bounce back from every obstacle and challenge that you faced. You fought a good fight, you finished the race, you kept the faith. Your victory over every adversity in your life gave me the inspiration to write this book. Like Momma, like son, we are two sides of the same victorious coin! I love you Mother!

Acknowledgements

To Dr. Romana Goplolan, you were my primary care physician for more than twenty years. You gave me the compassionate patient care that I needed during my medical history. Thank you for permitting me to be a partner with you in deciding my medical options. Thank you for allowing me to advocate for my own health and well being.

To Dr. Arshpreet Kaur, Division of Endocrinology-Sinai Hospital thank you for being the most compassionate and sensitive Doctor I have ever met. The first time I met you, I discerned your commitment to help me get well and stay healthy. I remember how you would smile when reading my lab results. You always encouraged me to keep up the good work. I love my appointments with you and I always anticipate the next appointment. You are a wonderful Doctor and a beautiful person.

To my Endocrinology Nurse, thank you for being patient with me and teaching me how to test my blood sugar level. Thank you for monitoring my blood sugar level charts and informing me that the prognosis for discontinuing insulin was good. Not only was it good, it came to pass. The Doctor discontinued the insulin about three months after I started taking it. I have been getting normal BSL readings everyday and I'm loving it.

To my Diabetes Resource Specialist, thank you for giving me good advice on dietary matters. You made me feel like an elementary school student reviewing the four food groups. You impressed upon me the importance of measuring the carbs in each meal, watching my salt and sugar intake and keeping up with my exercise routine. I especially enjoyed the time when you informed me that I could increase my carbohydrate intake. My wife and my daughter are still waiting for a written notice to certify your recommendation and approval of more carbs (L.O.L.)

To Dr. Jonathan Dubin, Baltimore Heart Associates P.A., thank you for believing in medical miracles. Thank you for sharing your testimony about the miracle you experienced as a young boy in growing up in New York City. You inspired me more than you know.

To my Urologist, thank you for helping to relieve my fear concerning my prostrate condition. Before I was referred to you, I had received a PSA reading from an insurance company medical Doctor that was off the charts. I consulted you for a second opinion and your test results proved that the insurance company's findings were incorrect; Big time! Thank you for having a finger that is patient friendly (L.O.L.).

To Dr. Thuy Vu Strong. OD Optometrist, thank you for your compassion and professionalism as you diagnosed and treated the Glaucoma that had developed in my eyes. Instead of the condition becoming progressively worse, it became progressively better. Thank you for informing me that the prognosis looked great for the future. Thank you for listening patiently to my story during one of my appointments at your office. You were expecting you fourth child at the time and I know that you probably preferred to listen to your baby's heart beat at the time (L.O.L.).

To my Ophthalmologist, thank you for performing laser eye surgery to successfully stop the progression of Glaucoma. Thank you for getting it right the first time. I don't plan on seeing you again (no pun intended).

To my Nephrologist, thank you for being candid with me about my kidney functioning. You gave me enough good news to off-set the not so good news. You informed me that my kidneys had been injured, but that the prognosis was good for a healthy future. The appointment with you on August 8, 2017 was the bomb! The battery of lab test results indicated that I was in a good place. I will continue to follow your orders and drink plenty of water.

To Pauline and Nikeya, a mother and daughter from St. Thomas, Virgin Islands, who came to the United States and were mentored by my wife. We adopted these two ladies into our family. They are examples of surviving and thriving against all odds. Pauline and Nikeya have overcome the devastation of several major Hurricanes in their homeland and have continued to press forward in life. They were there for me when I suffered my medical emergency on November 25, 2016. I was blessed when they visited me on November 24, 2017, the eve of the first anniversary of my hospitalization. We had a "Trauma To Triumph" party to celebrate the awesomeness of God in our lives.

To Morgan State University Toastmasters Club #979269, thank you for allowing me to sit in on several of your meetings where I heard some of the most creative and articulate speakers give five minute speeches to standing ovations. This experience inspired me to step up my game as a preacher of the Gospel. My sermons have become more creative and arresting because of the points I gleaned from all of the toastmaster speakers. Thank you Morgan Toastmasters.

INTRODUCTION

This book depicts the story of my life from as far back as I can remember, from the age of eight to my current age of sixty-three. The book chronicles the challenges, tragedies and life threatening medical conditions that invaded my life from childhood to manhood. The book highlights my epic battle against all odds.

Hindsight vision has persuaded me that the reason that I am alive today is primarily because of the Love, Grace, Mercy, Power and Providence of all mighty God. I have come to know the God who revealed himself in The Holy Scriptures (i.e., The Bible). My experiences with God during twelve life threatening medical conditions are detailed in this this book. I experienced three additional medical conditions, but they did not progress to a life-threatening state. I refer to God in the book as the "Unbeatable God". My unbeatable God has enabled me to survive and thrive in the midst of seemingly incredible odds. I would be remiss if I did not mention the fact that the Lord assigned eight compassionate and caring Doctors to treat my medical conditions. Each Doctor treated me according their particular specialty, while respecting the treatment options form the other Doctors. By the way, as far as I know, none of my Doctors personally collaborated with one another about my medical files. God also assigned many compassionate and caring health professionals from Sinai Hospital and the Life Bridge Health Center to assist in my recovery and follow up.

I was surrounded by a host of human angels. I was blessed with an All-Star medical team that helped me to survive and thrive "Against All Odds".

This book aims to be informative, instructive and inspirational. It was written over the course of 12 months from beginning to end. It was written with pristine transparency and honesty. But more importantly the book was crafted on a faith-based and biblical foundation. I could not have written this book at the age of twenty or fifty. The scope and sequence of my life experiences had to be reported from age eight to sixty-three in order for the reader to see the journey of an ordinary man on the road of resiliency and empowerment by the providential work and guidance of God. A Christian writer wrote that "Life is lived forward but understood backwards". At age sixty-two the Lord revealed to me that the worse things that could happen in my life had already happened. I could never have imagined at the age of eight the path my life would take over the span of fifty-four years.

Therefore, I was able to write this autobiographical sketch with a precise and accurate account of the historical facts. I invite the reader to take a look into the life of a miracle man who survived against the odds and is now thriving in life. I believe that I have already won every future battle in my life. There might be a setback in my future, but I believe that even with a future set back, I will survive and overcome again because my best days are still ahead of me. I live like I have a lifetime annuity of Grace and Mercy. I can have this kind of attitude because I am living out my destiny with the unbeatable God! I live depending on God for everything, but I work and strive like everything depends on me. I pray with folded hands, but immediately after the prayer I roll up my sleeves, tie my shoes and start walking steadily on the road revealed by God. The first sign that I read on the road was this: "Dear friend, I pray that you may enjoy good health and that all may go well with you, even as your soul is getting along well". (3 John verse 2: NIV).

Chapter 1

HOME SWEET HOME

SIX-TWENTY SAINTS ANN'S AVE.
BALTIMORE MARYLAND, 21218.

In 1960 this was the address and the home of an entire extended family in one house. I was about eight years young at the time. I could never figure out exactly how many relatives were living in that house, but my grandparents believed in taking care of family and making sure everyone had a place to live. The house provided shelter for three families consisting of three adults and eight children. Add four single adults with no children and my grandparents and we had a full house.

It was a packed house, but it was also a sweet home in the hood. Nobody got jealous about someone else's success, nobody lacked basic necessities. No child ever sassed an Elder.

The children rarely got to see and hold an actual dollar Bill. We became very familiar with change (penny, nickel, dime). If one of the kids was fortunate enough to possess a quarter, he or she was deemed extra special. While the children rarely saw cash in the hands of the elders, we always had food on the table, an ice cream cone after supper, or a treat while gathered in front

1

of the television on Saturday night to watch the Twilight Zone or the Alfred Hitch-cox Show. Six-Twenty Saint Ann's *Ave.* was a sweet place to live.

"Three Loose Cigarettes"

It was on a hot summer day when I was interrupted from my play-time to run an errand for my aunt Inez (a.k.a., little bits). She handed me 15 cents and told me to go to the neighborhood store to purchase three loose cigarettes.

Auntie assured me that I was mature enough (age 8) to cross 25th Street and return home safely. She said if there's any change left over you can use it to buy some sweets. With the thought of candy on my mind I walked out of the house, skipped down Saint Ann's Ave. and ran across 25th Street until I was met head on by an automobile that seem to come out of no where. There was no logical reason to explain why I survived that accident.

My aunt never received her three loose cigarettes and I never received my candy. But we did receive a miracle from God.

After three surgeries and three months in the hospital I became the miracle boy. I enjoyed being served like a King!

Even in an over crowded house my family created a place just for me. I was overwhelmed by the amount of compassion my family demonstrated to me during my time of suffering and healing.

All seventeen of my relatives loved on me in their own special way.

One day I walked out of the house, returned to school, reunited with my friends and rejoiced with my family. Something good had come out of what appeared to be a tragedy.

"Exodus from The Hood"

Typically, most African Americans leave the hood by means of upward mobility, an economic boost (good paying job), education achievement, hard work, or a helping hand from someone in the extended family.

Some families got an opportunity to move from the hood to an Improved hood. An improved hood is a black neighborhood that has less poverty, less crime, and less loitering, but on any given day one could experience the reality of the hood. As I reflect back on life at six-twenty Saint Ann's Ave. I can say that we did live in the "improved hood"

At the age of ten I witnessed the beginning of an Exodus from the house.

The Exodus started soon after the death of my grandmother (Julia Colbert).

She had struggled with a lengthy illness but she passed away peacefully.

It was not until the Home Going Service that the family really understood the kind woman they had been living with for so long.

She was more than just grandma, she was a woman of powerful faith.

As the Pastor gave the Eulogy the family sat spell-bound listening to the acts of kindness and love grandma demonstrated to family, neighbors, and strangers. I sat in the church, listening to a sermon for the first time, attending a funeral for the first time, hearing about faith for the first time. Realizing that it was my grandma's faith that held an entire family together in one small house, It was as if grandma Julia had a conversation with each of her adult children to prepare them for what to do when she passed.

Within a span of about five years all of the adult family members and their children moved to other houses. I can't recall who left first, second, or third, but I do remember that my grand-daddy (Bernard Colbert) was one of the last family members to remain at six-twenty Saint Ann's Ave. Rumor has it that Grand-daddy may have evicted the tribe after grandma Julia passed.

I do know that some families moved West and others remained on the east side. Eventually, Grandpa left the house vacant and moved in with a friend. I Currently live five minutes from Six-twenty Saint Ann's Ave. The house is no longer there, But I like to drive by that vacant lot and remember where I came from.

At age 9 we moved to the Westside of town. My mother ventured out on her own for the first time. My mother was a single parent with six children to care for. She found housing in the hood.

This hood was different from the Saint Ann's Ave. neighborhood we used to live in. Our new address was 538 Mission Court. There was only one block of Mission court with five small two-story row houses. My mother continued grandma's tradition of doing more with less and we prospered in the hood despite the fact the odds were stacked against us. We survived on welfare food and a welfare check; coal furnace heating in the winter and fans and window screens in the summer. There was the only one hospital in in Baltimore that was designated to treat blacks when we were growing up in the early nineteen-sixties.

We did have medical assistance provided by the Department of Social Services. The emergency room lines were always long and it seemed like the doctors and the medical Staff did not really care whether or not negroes survived life-threatening trauma and illness. I remember having a fever of 106 degrees from pneumonia. My mother treated my fever with lots of ice cubes, potato skins, and onions. She kept me wrapped in a thick blanket. She rocked me in her arms all night until the fever went down slightly.

She decided to take me to another hospital across town and the hospital treated me with penicillin. I had a bad reaction to the medicine. The hospital discharged me and gave my mother instructions for home care. My mother continued to pray and hold me in her arms until the fever broke. My mother became my hero and I discovered at the age of nine that a mother's love was the most powerful medicine in the world.

Moncy only circulated on the first of each month in the hood.

My mother had just enough to pay the Land-lord, the bill collector, and the Life Insurance man. Whatever little money remained was stretched out over thirty days until the next welfare check. My mother used the Lay-away plan to purchase our clothes, shoes, furniture and toys. She would start paying on back to school clothes and Christmas toys six months to a year in advance. We also received used clothing also known as "Hand-Me-Downs".

Each sibling handed down clothes to the younger siblings when they had out-grown their clothes. Like the family in the T.V. sit-com "Good Times", we had our own good times in the hood.

But life was different at St. Ann's Ave. We did not have to depend on welfare while living with our grandparents. Grand-daddy worked his entire life at Bethlehem Steel. He provided for everyone in the house. When we lived at St. Ann's Ave., we did not know we were poor until someone told us we were poor. Everyone had enough food to eat, enough to clothes to wear, enough family to love and enough room to grow. In the new house we realized that for the first time we had to get used to not having enough. The relevant question for the new hood was; "What do you do with the little that you have"? You Stretch It!

When the neighbors who had jobs ran out of money to buy basic food items like cheese, milk, flour, sugar, and butter, my Mom did not hesitate to send a neighbor a cup of this or that.

The same neighbors whose children teased us about being on welfare.

No one could convince us that we were poor, especially those neighbors who needed a helping hand. Me and my siblings became a part of the local Church while we were living on Mission Court. My mother never attended church with us. She sent us to church every Sunday dressed properly, and Mom gave us a quarter to put in the church offering plate. I remember there was a grocery store on the corner of Laurens St. and Etting St. that we used to go to before we attended Sunday School.

On several occasions me, my brother and my sisters would keep the quarter offering money and spend it at the corner store. One Sunday we schemed a plan to keep our offering and save it to buy candy after church.

The scheme went like this: we attached bubble gum between a quarter and an index finger. When the usher passed the offering basket to us, we would tap the inside of the offering plate with the quarter piece so the coin sounded like it had dropped into the offering plate. However, when the finger was withdrawn from the plate, the quarter piece would still be stuck to the finger.

Immediately after Church we would run to down the corner store and buy candy with stolen funds. We were convicted when the Pastor preached from Malachi 3:8; King James Version (KJV), "Will a man rob God?..."

The looming question that haunted us for many years was why didn't Momma attend church with her children? Momma wanted us to get right with Jesus. She believed that she had committed a multitude of transgressions in her life and she still had some skeletons in her closet. Momma wanted her children to grow up in the Church and live good Christian lives. The same Jesus she sent us to meet was the same Jesus she had met for herself.

My Mom's personal struggles kept her from going to church with her children until later in her life.

"A Bigger House In The Hood"

Me and my three siblings were getting older and my mother wanted to re-unite all six of the children together. Two of my sisters went to live with relatives when we moved from Saint Ann's Ave. They rejoined the family at Mission Court, but we only had two bedrooms in the small row house.

Two of my sisters shared a room with Mom and the other four children slept in one bed in the other room.

My mother managed to secure a larger house three blocks up the street form our current location at Mission Court. This was one of the most exciting times of our lives. All six siblings living together in one house with four bedrooms. The address was twenty-forty-five Division St.

A three story brick house located in the hood. I remember vividly how every one participated in the move. We moved in shifts, packing big items like mattresses and an "ice box" (a facsimile of a refrigerator with hot ice).

We placed everything we owned on three food market shopping carts and we carried smaller household items by hand. We pushed those shopping carts three blocks to our new home. We hustled all day and all night to finally get a piece of the pie.

Chapter 2

DON'T COUNT ME OUT!

It only took a week to discover that the grass was not greener on the other side of the hood and that Bigger don't necessarily mean better. One thing we did learn was that everybody was trying to do their best to survive in a dog eat dog neighborhood. Very few people I met in the neighborhood had any aspirations to do anything great in their lives.

Regardless as to whether you were included among the working class people or the welfare recipients, if you lived in the hood you had to learn how to survive the conditions that sought to keep you down. Poverty, crime, drug addiction, generational family dysfunction and a dog eat dog mentality were the primary culprits designed to keep me down in the hood. My pastor, (Bishop Walter Scott Thomas Sr.) would say in some of his sermons," some people have been down so long getting up never crosses their mind". Circumstances in the hood took me down to bad places where I stayed longer than I had intended to stay, went further then I had intended to go and paid more then I had intended to pay. Like a heavy weight fighter the hood beat me down in the boxing ring of life and it looked like I was being counted out.

I remember the day my high school physical education teacher pushed me into ten feet of water. My P.E. teacher (the late John Nash), had given me lessons on how to swim, but I refused to swim in deep water.

He told me that I could be a good swimmer if I could overcome my fear of drowning. When the teacher pushed me into the water I went into panic mode.

But then I realized that I had been taught how to submerge from the bottom of the pool and tread water once I reached the top. I instantly put into practice what I was taught. This was not the time for trial and error. I had to get it right the first time. To my own amazement I implemented what I learned and resurfaced to the top of the water to discover that my teacher was waiting for me with a safety pool-hook used to pull swimmers out of the water. I grabbed the hook and Mr. Nash pulled me to the side of the pool.

I lifted myself out of the pool and we both laughed hardily at the situation.

You see my teacher had confidence in the fact that I had learned how to avoid drowning and that the only way I would apply what I learned was to force me into the water. When I found myself hopelessly drowning in life, getting up did cross my mind and getting up stayed on my mind. I was on my way back.

I was down but not out!

I have more than enough "down but not out" stories.

I was knocked down by physical assaults from so called friends. One of my homies shot at me with his father's gun because I teased him for being a Momma's boy. He got so angry with me that he ran into his house and returned yielding a small hand gun. Fortunately, I had the sense to run before he returned with the gun. He proceeded to fire one shot at me from a distance of about fifty feet. The bullet miraculously hit a clothing line pole that I just happened to be standing in front of. The bullet was meant to hit me, but it hit the pole instead. A clothing-line pole probably saved my life. How could I ever imagine that a pole the size of a broom stick would protect me from a bullet.

What if the pole was not there? I could have been killed that day.

God saved my life with a pole. An angry friend tried to take me out but God blocked the bullet with a pole.

At the age of fifteen I received my first drink of alcohol. Colt 45 Malt Liquor was the drink of choice. Although my mother forbid Me and my siblings from drinking alcoholic beverages, there was a season of her life in which she abused alcohol. After a night of hard drinking my mother decided to put what was left of the alcohol in the refrigerator to be kept for another time.

This was the first time I had ever seen alcohol in the "Ice box".

On that night curiosity got the best of me and I found my self sipping from the bottle of Colt 45. To be exact, the sip was one bottle top of beer. One bottle top of alcohol was all it took to get me drunk. I never told my mother what I did that night, it was my secret. What started in private eventually became public. That one sip of alcohol progressed to one can, one quart, a six pack, wine, and almost any other alcoholic beverage I could get my hands on. I consumed alcohol frequently from age fifteen to age thirty (fifteen years). Never once did I consider myself an alcoholic and no one ever called me an alcoholic.

Some people can take one drink of alcohol land never drink alcohol again, on the other hand, with certain people one drink is too many and a million drinks is not enough!

Alcohol became my best friend. I drank alcohol at the party, I drank alcohol on the street corner with my buddies.

I drank alcohol before a date, I drank alcohol to feel good, I drank alcohol while watching the football game on T.V.

I drank alcohol after the playing pick-up basketball at the neighborhood recreation center. At times I would drink myself into a stupor, fall down on the ground, crawl up the steps to my house, make my way up to my third floor bed room and crash on the floor with my clothes still on.

I became what the psychologist refer to as a functioning alcoholic.

I watched many of my friends and relatives bow down to alcohol.

I wondered for a long time why alcohol did not take me out.

But now I know why I survived. It was God's amazing grace!

But there was still another enemy behind the bushes waiting to ambush my life. The enemy's name was Heroin. I used heroin religiously for five years of my life. I started out sniffing the stuff and later graduated to the needle.

No one among my family or friends was willing to believe that I was addicted to heroin. I did not have the profile of an addict. But what I did have was private pain that cried out for relief. The relief came in form of heroin.

Heroin became my prescription for pain.

The prescription called for one shot a day or as needed. The heroin epidemic was so powerful in the hood to the extent that when news spread that someone died of an over dose of the poison, all the junkies in the hood rushed to the dealer to obtain the same dope that had just killed a friend or family member. Their reasoning was if one bag of the dope is powerful enough to cause someone to overdose and die, just a little of the same stuff would not kill someone, but it would make someone feel super good. I was employed by the Baltimore City Public School System for five years with an active Heroin addiction. I was able to buy drugs on my modest teacher salary. I did not steal, rob or kill to get Heroin. I used my own money to support my habit.

But some things had to be cut short or cut out in order for me to finance my addiction. (e.g., rent, food, bills, provision for my family).

My wife was the one who kept the family from collapsing. she stood by me through thick and thin, in the best of times and the worst of times. She hated what my addiction was doing to the family, but she never stopped loving me and she hoped and prayed everyday that God would rescue our family from the torment and devastation of my Heroin addiction that was holding me as a hostage.

I had the will to stop using drugs, but I did not know the way to quit.

"For I know that good itself does not dwell in me, that is, in my sinful nature. For I have the desire to do what is good, but I cannot carry it out. For I do not do the good I want to do, but the evil I do not want to do -- this I keep on doing. Now if I do what I do not want to do, it is no longer I who do it, but it is the sin living in me that does it".

A man named Paul was inspired to write these words in the Book of Romans 7:18-20; New International Version (NIV). I thought to myself, if a great man of God like Paul felt Helpless at a point in his life as a Christian, who was I to think hopelessness wouldn't find me at my address. I reached a point where I was sick and tired of being sick and tired of this monkey hanging on my back. One morning I got out of the bed at about five a.m. and decided I was going to get some help.

I left my house with the same determination that I had when I chased down the drug dealer to cop some dope. This time I was running for my help.

One of my partners in crime referred me to a methadone program in East Baltimore. He told me I had to get to the program by Six A.M. and get in line. He said don't procrastinate because they take the first fifty in line.

He added, make sure you are "dirty" when you go to the program (that is; have some fresh drugs in your system). The clinicians will draw your blood to determine if you are a real drug abuser. If no drugs are found in your system, you will not qualify for the methadone program.

I had no problem qualifying for the program. I was the tenth person in line and high as a kite. I did what I had to do to get some help. But what I thought would help me, only frustrated me. I discovered that the program only provided methadone treatment for three days. All the long-term treatment programs had a waiting list. How could the medical experts think that five years of drug abuse could be healed with three doses of methadone. It was like feeding a whale three small fish and expecting the fish to satisfy the whale's appetite. I took the treatment for three days; it helped to relieve the physical pain associated with withdrawal from drug addiction, but after the three day trial was over, the pain returned. I resorted to buying methadone from street hustlers.

After about a year of drinking the "met" (street name for methadone), It felt like I had jumped out of the frying pan and into the fire.

The met had its own brand of unhealthy side effects. Methadone was a legal substitute for heroin. Its purpose was to stop the pain associated with withdrawal from drug addiction.

Once the pain issue was resolved, one could begin to rehabilitate his or her life. Eventually, I stopped taking the methadone because of its long-term health risks. What Now! I was afraid to surrender myself to a long-term in-patient treatment facility, so I stepped out on faith and asked the Lord to heal me from the disease of heroin addiction.

The Lord answered my prayer. He took me on a journey that led to Healing and the full recovery of my life.

To God be the Glory, he has enabled me to live a drug free life for the past thirty years. I escaped the bullet, the bottle, and bags of poison, but there was yet another monster that tried to conquer my soul (depression). I discovered that the depression was not in the alcohol or the heroin, the problem was in my human sin nature. Human beings are born with a propensity, proclivity, inclination and an attraction to sin. To sin is to rebel, reject or go beyond the boundaries of God's holy, righteous, just and loving laws for life and well-being.

Human beings are naughty by nature and find themselves enticed and held captive to things that are too legit to quit. The lyrics in certain rap culture music underscores the basic principle of human sin perfectly.

Committing sin does not cause God to love human kind any less than he has always loved us. Yes, God is displeased with us when we sin, but he does not abandon us when we sin. There are consequences for sin and one of the greatest consequences is premature death. But for the grace of God, any one of a thousand sins that I had committed could have killed me.

When I think about all the terrible things that could have happened to me because of sin, I absolutely know and believe that I survived "Against All Odds" by the Grace and Mercy of God. The problem is that some people fail to accept God's remedy for sin—Jesus's sacrificial and atoning death on the cross for forgiveness of sin.

My advice to any person is to stop making excuses for sin and accept the prescription that will bring forgiveness and healing. The question that some medical researchers grapple with is: Does drug abuse and/or alcohol abuse cause depression or does depression cause alcohol abuse and/or drug abuse?

Some medical researchers contend that the disease of depression is not caused by chemicals in alcohol or drugs but rather its root cause is a chemical in-balance in the brain. Drug and alcohol abuse becomes a means of self- medicating a disease. One can not drink a disease away. One needs a medical intervention, a therapeutic intervention and most of all a God intervention in order to deal with this malady. I used alcohol and drugs to treat my depression. I discovered that I was using the wrong prescription. I was driven to the point where I sought medical and psychiatric treatment to help with my chronic depression.

I was diagnosed at the age of thirty-two. I was prescribed medication that produced bad side effects. I tried to discontinue the medication on several occasions, but it only led to relapse.

I remember praying everyday to the Lord, please deliver me and heal me from this sickness. But the Lord did not take the disorder away. "Instead he said to me my grace is sufficient, my strength is made perfect in weakness".

I remember one day I decided to research the side effects of the medication. I read a statement that transformed my attitude about dealing with bad side effects. The statement read; "The benefits of this medication are greater than the side effects". I believe that side effects are simply irritations we must endure in order to receive benefits to enjoy.

God empowered me to live and thrive with a condition that was supposed to keep me mentally bound for life. Society has conditioned people to become fixated with fear when they are given a negative diagnosis from the Doctor, we have a tendency to focus on the negative diagnosis and fail to understand that even when the negative diagnosis creates a sense of hopelessness, the reality is that God can provide a positive prognosis.

The diagnosis gives the current reality about the condition, but the prognosis talks about the prospects of the condition (i.e.; how the condition might end-good or bad). The prognosis is a forecast of the probable course the condition might take. Depression was my diagnosis, but abundant life was my prognosis. God assured me in his word that no weapon formed against me would prosper. My mind was the intended target of the diagnosis, but God's prognosis for my condition was revealed to me in his word; "For I know the plans I have for you, declares the Lord, plans to prosper you and not to harm you, plans to give you hope and a future" -- Jeremiah 29:11, New International Version (NIV).

The negative diagnosis of mental illness came at age thirty-two, but the positive prognosis has prevailed even to the time of the writing of this book.

For thirty years the Lord has enabled me to live with and above a condition that was supposed to destroy my life. But the real miracle is that the Lord kept me in my right mind and caused my life to prosper.

On November 25, 2016 I was rushed to Sinai Hospital by ambulance and admitted after collapsing in my home. The doctors determined that I had a near fatal blood sugar level of 1100. I should not have arrived to the emergency room alive. But On December 8, 2016 I was discharged from Sinai Hospital after an eleven day stay. The medical treatment and the

Grace and Mercy of God enabled me to leave the hospital with a normal blood sugar level. I considered this to be a medical miracle because, my blood sugar level was so far above a normal BSL reading for an unknown period of time (I was blind-sided and shocked by this discovery).

The doctor also discontinued the medicine I was taking for Depression. I claim this as another miracle. I often wondered why God waited 30 years before he healed me of depression. But today I realized that God is God and beside him there is no one else. I learned to accept what God allows. But I also learned not to settle for anything less than God's best for my life. What matters most is that my life has been revived, my health has been restored, and my spirit has been renewed for such a time as this. However, I did leave the hospital with a diagnosis of two types of Diabetes. I dropped two pills and picked up two different kinds of medication. I was tempted to complain and tell God he was not being fair. But I quickly repented and remembered the miracles he had performed while I was in the hospital. However, pain was not through with me yet. I was diagnosed with Rheumatoid Arthritis about a month after I was released from the hospital.

It seemed like this ailment was waiting behind the bushes for the opportunity to ambush me and declare, "Got Yah". In my mind I yelled back at "Rheuma" and "Arthur" and said no! I have both of you in the palm of my hand". Ironically, it was my Mom who referred to her Rheumatoid Arthritis as "Rheuma and Authur". One day she was wrestling with the pain and inflammation caused by the disease and she said to me with a bit of humor; "Never let Rheuma and Arthur move in, because they will not want to leave". I thought to my self, God works in mysterious ways his wonders to perform. Maybe God has another miracle in store for the Diabetes and the Rheumatoid Arthritis. In the mean-time I remembered the Scripture in Job 14:14; "If a man die, shall he live again? All the days of my appointed time I will wait, till my change come"- King James Version (KJV).

A near fatal car accident, a 106 degree fever, a bullet that missed the target, alcohol and drug addiction, clinical depression, an enlarged prostrate, high blood pressure, glaucoma, two types of diabetes, Rheumatoid Arthritis and life in the hood tried to count me out. But I declared what David declared in Psalm 27:13-14 (KJV), "I had fainted, unless I had believed to see the goodness of the Lord in the land of the living; Wait on the Lord: be of good courage and he shall strengthen thine heart: wait, I say, on the Lord".

Chapter 3

TOLERATE YOUR BURDENS, BUT COUNT YOUR BLESSINGS

The Bible says in Romans 5:3-4 (NIV) "…but we also glory in our Sufferings, because we know that suffering produces perseverance; perseverance, character; and character, hope. *Notice that this verse does not say that we should rejoice for our sufferings, but in our sufferings.* I remember reading a Corie ten Boom line, "Thank God for the fleas". The fleas kept the German soldiers out of the barracks in the in the concentration camp where she was imprisoned. This allowed her to minister and visit with those who were being persecuted. There she could show and share Jesus. Corie ten Boom was not thanking God for the suffering, she was thanking God for the fleas that kept the German soldiers away from the prison thus allowing her to minister to her people in the concentration camp.

I want to revisit a statement I made earlier in this book; "the benefits of taking this medicine is greater than the side effects of the medicine".

This statement is included with every prescription. I used to become paranoid whenever I read about the multiple and potential life threatening side effects that accompanied the medicine I was prescribed. But now I understand that if you want the blessing that the medication may bring, you also have to tolerate the side effects of the medication. No one lives a pain-free life. Even the best life will have to endure periodic trials or life's irritations. People who fail to endure hardships will miss the blessing that the hardship was intended to produce. The Bible says "For his anger lasts only a moment, but his favor lasts a lifetime; weeping may endure for a night, but joy rejoicing comes in the morning" (Psalm 30:5 NIV).

Interpretation: The Lord will not leave you to perish in the mid-night of your experience. Just as Mid-night signifies the ending of a day, morning indicates the dawning of a new day. Like-wise God promises that there is a set time for deliverance from pain and suffering.

No one in his or right mind enjoys pain. But some people believe they are strong enough to drink pain without a chaser. The delusional G.I. Joes' and Rambos' of this world glory in their ability to bear pain with a smile and see their pain as a virtue that will be rewarded in heaven.

But the Bible says: "Blessed is the one who perseveres under trial, because having stood the test, that person will receive the crown of life that Lord has promised to those who love him" (James 1:12 NIV).

I hope that at this point in my story you have ascertained that I have endured seasons of incredible pain in my life. It seemed to me like pain had signed a long-term lease in my body.

But the Bible records: "fixing our eyes on Jesus, the pioneer and perfecter of our faith. For the joy set before him, he endured the cross, scorning its shame, and sat down at the right hand of the throne of God" (Hebrews 12:2 NIV). Interpretation: While Jesus was enduring the unbelievable pain of the crucifixion, he was looking ahead to all of the lives that would be changed as a result of his sacrifice for the sins of mankind.

Nothing can compare to the humiliation, scorn and torture Jesus suffered on that old rugged cross, and no one can imagine the inner joy he possessed despite the fact that there was no evidence at the cross to show that he had any reason to expect anything good as a result of his tremendous suffering.

The best analogy I can offer to describe Jesus' suffering on the Cross is that of an expectant mother to be in the throes of labor pains.

She endures the labor pains for the bundle of joy that is set before her.

Expectant mothers down through the ages have endured labor pains multiple times. For the joy; the life, the gift from God, that the gynecologist or the midwife places in front of the woman in the delivery room, the bedroom or in the back seat of a car or cab, that expectant mother will endure the pain. We can learn a lesson from an expectant mother: Tolerate your burdens, but don't forget to count your blessings!

Chapter 4

COINCIDENCE OR PROVIDENCE

During my adolescence life and part of my young adulthood, I was convinced that certain events and relationships I had encountered were mere coincidences. But at around the age of thirty-two, I learned that there was a distinct difference between the two experiences. According to the dictionary a coincidence is an occasion when two or more things happen at the same time, especially in a way that is unexpected or unlikely.

On the other hand providence is defined as a manifestation of divine care or direction or the protective care of God or of nature as a spiritual power. In the case of coincidence, one does not understand how circumstances are connected or aligned with the big picture or purpose in life. People who accept some of the things that happen in their lives as mere coincidences may not be able to comprehend a sovereign and omniscient God who is in control of everything at all times without violating one's free will or manipulating the course of nature. Rather in the case of providence God allows one to make choices, but in the grand scheme of things the choices one makes, good or bad eventually work together to accomplish God's ultimate purpose.

With providence two wrong choices can equal a right choice because God is the superintendent over our choices without ever violating our free-will. On the other hand in the case of coincidence one fails to see that the dots or events of life have been pre-ordained to form a complete picture.

But with providence, the dots in and of themselves do not reveal a complete picture until one starts to connect the dots.

God has set in place the dots in our lives, we simply move from dot to dot; event to event, circumstance to circumstance according to our human will and when all the dots have been connected we see the big picture or purpose. The next time you meet someone in a mall, at an event, or on the other side of the planet it won't be because you just happened to be in the same place at the same time without any apparent purpose; but I believe that the dots in your life are being providentially connected to accomplish God's purpose in your life.

To bring home the reality and the concept of "Divine Providence" in the most clear and concise manner, I offer the reader this analogy; Divine Providence functions like a "GPS" device (Global Positioning System). One may enter a particular destination into the system and at some point along the route the individual might make a mistake and take a wrong turn. The GPS will not alert the driver about the wrong turn, instead the GPS device will re-route the driver and give the driver correct directions from the location of the wrong turn.

In addition, the GPS will give the driver the fastest path to the Intended destination from the place where the wrong turn was made.

In this way the driver can never be lost even if the individual continues to make wrong turns. The person driving will probably get to the destination later than expected, but they will eventually get to the intended destination. The individual will eventually get to their destination in "Chronos time". Mckinley Valentine writes that Chronos is one of two Greek words that refers to time. Chronos means chronological or sequential time (i.e., clock time). Mckinley goes on to write that God works in 'Kairos time' (i.e., outside of time). Kairos time is the second Greek word for time. Kairos is a word that signifies a period or season of time, a moment of indeterminate time in which an event of significance happens. Where Chronos is quantitative, kairos is qualitative. It measures moments, not seconds; furthermore, it refers to the right moment, the opportune moment, the perfect moment. The world takes a breath, and in the pause before it exhales, fates can be changed".

How many times have we heard these words from a preacher:

"God may not be there when you want him, but he is always on time". or "God is never too early and he is never too late, but he is always there when you need him". Providence says one might be late in Chronos time, but exactly on time in Kairos time. One always arrives on time and on purpose. It's not by coincidence but by providence!

Now let me share some of the providential workings of God in my life. These things happened right on time and on purpose without me understanding that I was cooperating with God to bring about his purpose for my life.

Case Study #1

In 1998 we embarked on a journey to purchase our first home.

We were confronted with a problem. We were scheduled to move Into our new home in March, however; the lease on our townhouse did not expire until June, the rental manager informed us that if we moved out of the townhouse in March, we would still owe three months rent unless the townhouse was leased by another tenant by the end of March. The rental agent informed us that as of March 25th, no one had applied to sign the lease on our townhouse and we were Scheduled to move into the new house on March 31st. We could not afford to pay the remaining three months rent left on our lease agreement.

On March 26th my wife was discussing our dilemma with her co-worker and another co-worker sitting near-by over heard the conversation.

The ease dropping co-worker just happened to be searching for a three bed-room townhouse for her family and she inquired of my wife about the townhouse that we were trying to leave.

To make a long story short, my wife informed the co-worker about our current situation and encouraged the co-worker to visit the rental agent and inform her about her knowledge of a townhouse that would be available on March 31st. The co-worker visited the rental agent on March 27th and signed a lease to move into our vacated townhouse on April 1st1998. We moved out on March 31st and moved into our new home on March 31st and the rest is history (or shall I say Providence!).

CASE STUDY #2

I could have never imagined or predicted the process that God guided me through in meeting and marrying the woman I fell in love with. I was 12 years old and she was 9 years old when we met. Eva lived two houses down from my house in the twenty hundred block of Division Street. I first met my future wife like most black kids meet in an inner-city neighborhood; socializing and engaging in black cultural activities.

It was during a game called "hide and seek" that I laid eyes on a beautiful little short girl with a brown sugar complexion and ebony eyes accented with an aroma of sweet innocence.

I was always able to find little Eva because she would always hide in the same spot each time we played the game. It was as if she only wanted me to find her each time. We were certainly not mature enough at the time to develop a serious relationship, but the game provided a wonderful opportunity to fantasize and gaze into a potential future relationship. However; there was one scenario that challenged the reality of a future relationship with Eva. Eva had an older sister who had a crush on me. Her sister was 12 years old so it seemed as if we had something in common. But as it turned out age was the only thing we had in common. I don't know to this day if Eva's oldest sister was aware of the crush I had on Eva, but I kept it a secret in my heart.

The last thing I wanted was a family feud over a dude, so I had what I called a play relationship with the big sister and I kept the possibility of a real future relationship with Eva close to my heart.

As time went by I graduated from Douglass High School and left Eva behind in the 9th grade. I had relationships with other girls during a span of five years after graduation. During that time Eva had graduated from high school and enrolled at Harcum Community College in Philadelphia P.A. I was attending the Community College of Baltimore on a basketball scholarship. It just so happened that things did not work out for Eva at Harcum and she returned home after one year. That's when our paths crossed again and one thing led to another. We started dating and we fell in love for real. We eventually got married after eight years of developing an unbreakable bond of love. God guided our lives over a span of eight years of causal interactions and brought us together to complete what he had already ordained for us. The dots were connecting that God had providentially set in place before we had ever laid eyes on one another.

I will always believe that our union was never a coincidence, but a divinely orchestrated plan ordered by God to accomplish his purpose in our lives.

Did I think It was a possibility that I could have chosen a woman other than Eva to fall in love with?--Yes I did, but I am fully confident that it was the providential working of God in our lives that prevailed over all the possibilities and the probabilities of either one us choosing someone else to fall in love with. We make choices, but God has the sovereign power to make the ultimate choice when we yield to his ways and his purposes in our lives.

For thirty-nine years our marriage relationship has shown evidence that God ordered our steps and worked all things together for our good according to his purpose for us.

Case Study #3

If someone had told me in 1972 (the year I graduated from Douglass High School) that I would become the principal of the renowned *Paul Laurence Dunbar High School* in Baltimore Md., I would have probably called that person crazy or believed that they were under the influence of a hallucinogenic drug. But most of all I would have taken the comment as an insult to my Intelligence.

Never in my wildest imagination did I even conceive of a career in the field of education. No one in my family ever told me that I had the potential to achieve something great in life. I believed that the best I could do in life was to become a policeman, a fireman, or an athlete. I had no role models or examples of success in my immediate or extended family structure. But I did have honest, hard working people in my life who told me that I would only get out of life what I was willing to put into life. No one in my family had remotely thought about achieving any education beyond High School.

The majority of my relatives settled for a ninth or tenth grade education at Paul Laurence Dunbar High School.

It's amazing how God providentially guided me through my educational process and elevated me to become the principal of a school that my mother, my grandparents, my aunts and my uncles attended. God favored me to ascend to what I call the pinnacle of success in my life. I jokingly tell people that God did not allow me to attend Dunbar because I might have followed in the path of some my family members and failed to graduate.

God guided me to Douglass High School in West Baltimore where I graduated and became the first person in my family to attend and graduate from college (I reckon there will be some family members who will fact check this claim). What's more amazing is that fact that I had no inclination or inspiration to even fill out a college application. But in spite of my lack of confidence in my intellectual ability, I enrolled at the Community College of Baltimore in the fall of 1972. My motivation was not guided by academic pursuits, but by a tremendous zeal for the sport of basketball. My love for Basketball Kept me in Douglass High School for three years when I had little desire to get good grades. I was an All MSA (Maryland Scholastic Association) Basketball 3rd team selection in my senior year at Douglass. I was proud to make the 3rd team when the first team was comprised of Dunbar superstars like Skip Wise, Larry Gibson, Box Owens, and Billy Snowden.

I remember the most exciting game of my basketball career was a one point lost to Dunbar on our home court. One point was the closet a Douglass team had ever come to a victory over a Dunbar basketball team during the tenure of coach William

Sugar Cain. He was the legendary coach of the poets who set the stage for great coaches like Bob Wade and Pete Pompey.

Coach Jerry Phipps was the only coach who seriously recruited me out of High school and gave me an honest lecture about life, academics and basketball. I enjoyed my experience at the Community College of Baltimore.

My next stop was Bowie State College where again I was only recruited by one school to play college basketball. I was selected to the Baltimore Sun Sports writers "All Maryland College Basketball Team" at Bowie averaging nearly 20 points per game in my junior year. My GPA also improved to 3.2 mainly because I was living on campus and had lots of time to study.

The distractions were minimal at Bowie and my room mate Fred Wright, kept me accountable on the basketball court as well as in classroom at Bowie State College.

Next stop was Coppin State College where the legendary coach John Bates offered me a chance to finish my senior year at the West Baltimore N.A.I.A. basketball power house. I must confess that I did not plan on transferring to Coppin State College for my senior Year. However, I was forced to leave Bowie State College because I got into trouble with the law and consequently I was dismissed from the School. I thank God that I was able to side step a potential prison sentence. I received a pardon and coach Bates gave me another chance. He did not judge me, but he gave me what I consider to be one of the greatest opportunities of my life.

I got a chance to redeem myself and show coach Bates, Coppin State College, my friends and my family that I was a quality human being who was on a wonderful journey toward my destiny. I graduated from Coppin with a B.S. Degree in

Special education and ten years later I received a Master's Degree in Rehabilitation Counseling from Coppin.

I also earned a Graduate Certificate in Administration and Supervision from the Johns Hopkins University School of Professional Studies in Business and Education. All these accomplishments were achieved "Against all Odds".

But wait!, there's more; I was employed by the Baltimore City Public School System straight out of College in 1979 as a Special Education Teacher.

I worked my way up the ladder of success to positions in the areas of School Based Management and Central Office Administration. But the cream of the crop came when I was promoted from assistant principal at Paul Laurence Dunbar High School to the position of Principal (2008). It would have been impossible for me to write this script in advance. There was no way I could have logically conceived that any of these things would happen in my life.

The only thing I could do was to stay sane, except, and embrace what God was doing through his providential will and purpose in my life.

I close chapter 4 with one of the most profound Scriptures I have ever read in my life: "None of the rulers of this age understood it, for if they had, they would not have crucified the Lord of Glory. However, as it is written; no eye has seen, no ear has heard, no mind has conceived the things God has prepared for who love him-these things God has revealed to us by his Spirit. The Spirit searches all things, even the deep things of God" (I Cor. 2:8-10 NIV).

Chapter 5

NEVER WOULD HAVE MADE
IT WITHOUT HER

In his book, Why I Love Black Women, Michael Dyson bears witness to the glories of older women, the strength of the church women, and the heartaches of single women and urges us to all to honor the physical, intellectual and spiritual gifts of black women in society that is still dominated by white ideals of beauty. Now allow me introduce you to a woman who is the driving force in my life. My wife of 39 wonderful years. I believe Eva is the one woman God had in mind for me before I ever laid eyes on her. I truly fell in love with her at first sight. I dated other woman before I met Eva, but none of them arrested me and put me in a trance like Eva. I did not realize the type of woman she was until my life started to spin out of control a few years after we met. Although the all odds seemed to be against our staying together, she stuck with me like white on rice. She was my super glue. She literally rescued me from self-destruction and pre-mature death. She endured my craziness even in the midst of her own setbacks and challenges. She carried her own baggage as well as the garage full of issues that I hauled into her life. She loved me back to life.

She is definitely my better half. She is my help meet. She complements me in every imaginable way. Eva is my rib, my joy, my sine qua non (absolutely necessary), my raison d'etre (my reason for living) and my Pied a Terre (my hiding place). Eva puts the glide in my stride, she puts the pep in my step and the she is the tiger in my tank.

My wife is an original master piece created by God. God broke the mold after he designed Eva. She can be as gentle as a dove and on the flip side she can roar like a lioness. She is truthful, faithful and beautiful. Next to God no one holds me accountable like my wife. She knows how to get on my case and straighten me out when ever I get beside myself. We have been blessed to experience an extraordinary relationship for 39 years. We have survived some valleys, but our mountain top experiences have far out weighed our low moments. Eva means "life giving" and she has been sustaining my life for 39 years. The Bible says that "He who finds a wife finds what is good and he receives favor from the Lord" (Proverbs 18:22 NIV). Eva is the good wife who brings favor to my life. She did not do me a favor when I married her, she brought the favor of God to the relationship. In other words, my life was extraordinarily enriched because of the gifts and character traits she possessed in her life.

Favor is not earned, it is provided freely through the sovereignty of God. God's favor can not be gained by manipulation or intimidation, rather it is provided through the Grace of God. My wife has blessed my life with her life and there is no way I could earn her love or pay for the joy and contentment she brings to the relationship. I provide for her financially, emotionally and spiritually, but these things are not provided to win or earn her love. These things are merely fringe benefits. I am the husband that I am to my wife because she has made it so easy for me to love her. She bears my short comings and my weaknesses. What I lack in effort and ability is compensated by favor from my wife.

In Genesis God brought the woman Eve to Adam after he had taken her from Adam's side. When Adam first laid eyes on Eve he called her woman, bone of his bone and flesh of his flesh. Adam and Eve became united together as one entity. This is the essence of the marriage relationship. Adam was not alone anymore, he was united with a woman who was suitable for him, a wife who would help him become all that he needed to be. Adam became the husband his wife needed him to become.

Don't get it twisted, your mate was not created to fulfill all your need, only God can do that. Some married couples have been taught to believe a myth. They enter the marriage relationship each bringing fifty percent and expect their marriage to work. Soul singer Teddy Pendergass wrote a song about a 50/50 Love. Wrong thinking! - each partner has to bring one hundred percent of themselves to the relationship. In other words, one has to be whole in his or her single state of being before he or she can realistically expect to maintain a healthy marriage relationship.

I contend that divorce and separation in our society happens so frequently because individuals enter the sacred act of matrimony handicapped and afflicted from the start of the relationship. Society is filled with needy people who are expecting another imperfect human being to do what only God can do.

My advice to potential mates is to work on your own baggage before you say "I DO". If both partners are lacking wholeness and maturity before the marriage, they will be lacking after the marriage ceremony. The ceremony is not the marriage. It only lasts about for two hours. The marriage starts after the ceremony. The marriage requires a life time of love, work, commitment, forgiveness and favor.

Allow me to offer some keys to sustaining and enjoying a healthy and lasting marriage relationship:

1. Identify a list of things you would consider to be non-negotiable in a potential marriage relationship. Discuss these issues with your fiancé or potential marriage partner to ensure that both partners are on the same page concerning expectations and commitments in the relationship. I recommend that this be done only if both parties believe that the relationship is seriously headed toward the altar. This task can be accomplished during a candle-light dinner engagement or at home in the living room.

2. Do not assume anything, rather enter the relationship with an open mind.

Don't be naive, if the same question keeps popping up in your mind each time you are with your potential marriage partner, ask the question in a user friendly manner: for example, Do you want children? -- When?

How many? -- Would you feel unfulfilled if you were unable to have children?

Dr. Robin L Smith writes in her book Lies at the ALTAR; The truth About Great Marriages is that "many couples start with God in the center of the relationship and keep him there, but too many couples start with their own ideas and understanding of marriage. They start out with a token expression of God's involvement at the altar, but they gradually ease God out after a series of unresolved conflicts".

Don't stop speaking to your mate because you disagree on something. Speak to God alone in prayer about the problem, get his wisdom then come together at a mutually agreed upon time and place and discuss what God revealed to you about the problem. While you are waiting on God's guidance, talk about other topics of interest that you already agree on. I call this strategy communicating under protest or appeal. In other words, you agree to disagree until you get a ruling or decision from the Supreme Court (GOD!).

In closing this chapter, I contend that each potential marriage partner should bring a ton of forgiveness to the relationship. Forgiveness will be needed by both parties along the journey if each partner expects the relationship to be loving, sustainable and maturing. Some couples enter the relationship with the thrill of great expectations only to experience the agony of disappointment at some point. Some aspiring couples break up because they refuse to forgive even minor offenses. Major offenses will inevitably lead to irreconcilable differences. If neither partner is willing to give up his or her way in order to resolve a conflict, they might fail to understand and accept the fact that refusing to give up their ways to Christ might be the main issue that blocks forgiveness. It might be a situation where-by each partner has absolutely no intention of giving up certain things, not even to love. But if they are able to trust the Lord, there is hope for a Loving and lasting marriage relationship.

Chapter 6

TWO PRECIOUS GIFTS FROM HEAVEN

Children are gifts from God. Parents have been given the ability and equipment to reproduce and give birth, but God is the source and creator of life. He designed the DNA of every human being. Couples come together at the right time and turn on their equipment and boom, a new life is conceived. The truth of the matter is that a man and a woman can't create a baby. They participate in God's process of procreation. God commanded Adam and Eve to be fruitful and multiply.

As parents we have the ability to reproduce and the responsibility of raising our offspring as precious gifts from God. Unfortunately, there are some people who don't see children as gifts from God, but as objects generated from their own imaginations; consequently, some parents mistakenly believe that they alone own their children lock, stock and barrel.

My mother used said to say to me "boy! -- I brought you into this world and I can take you out of it". Parents can very well shorten the lives of their children, but only God can extend life. The sixth commandment informs us that children are required to honor their mother and father so that their days may be long upon the earth. This happens to be the only one of the Ten Commandments with a promise attached to it. On the other hand, fathers should not provoke their children to the point of anger. The Bible says -- "Father's, do not exasperate your children; instead, bring them up in the training and instruction of the Lord" (Ephesians 6:4 NIV). In other words, the father has the unique responsibility of ensuring that he does not provoke his children to the extent that they become rebellious and out of control.

Surely Mom has a part in this, but God is going to hold the father responsible for the task of raising the kids so that they honor both parents and not resent them. I whole heartily embraced my responsibilities as a father before my two children were born. I promised God and my wife that I would cherish and nourish my children with God's help and meet every challenge and situation in their lives with fatherly grace and wisdom. I made this commitment in part because I never laid eyes on my biological father. He abandoned me and my mother before I was born. My mother never told me anything about my father except for the fact that he was enlisted in the military. I spent most of my teenage life wondering about why the man who fathered me also rejected me as a gift from God. Did he really understand the precious gift that God had given to him?

I promised my Heavenly Father that I would never abandon nor forsake my children, rather I would love them with all my heart, strength, mind and soul.

I would raise them in the fear and admonition of the Lord. To the best of my ability I believe I have done so with pride and joy.

My first gift, Stacie Nicole; was born August 15, 1978. She is my precious, beautiful, and lovable bundle of joy. I believe I was the happiest man alive when I went to the hospital and saw my little baby girl wrapped in a blanket in her mother's arms. I held my precious bundle of joy close to my chest being careful not to squeeze her too tightly. This was my first time ever holding an infant.

I was afraid that I would do something wrong and ruin my first experience with my first child, but I managed to get through it without any problems.

As I held my baby girl I began to think about the awesome task that was cast before me as a father. I thought about so many things and situations that could possibly be included in raising a girl. In particular, I reflected on how my mother and my mother-in-law (Eva Anderson) raised their daughters. My four sisters and my wife's five sisters were products of the wisdom and courage of these two mothers.

I considered the parenting tactics of these Super Mothers and how they dealt with girl issues, and I also thought about me and my wife's convictions about raising a female child. I can proudly say that me and my wife came to an agreement that the wisdom and courage our Moms applied to parenting stood the test of time. We see the results today in our grown daughter and we don' regret how we raised our daughter. We embrace the good and the bad things that have shaped Stacie's life because we know that God caused all things to work together for her good.

Now I want to talk about some of the stories that emerged along the course of my daughter's journey to womanhood. As you read this account please keep in mind that Stacie is the epitome of the term "Daddy's Little Girl". Let's start with Stacie's transition from elementary school to middle school. She qualified to attend one of the top middle schools in the Baltimore. However, she decided that she did not want to attend the school because her friends were scheduled to attend another middle school. It was not a poor choice, but it was not the best choice as far as me and my wife was concerned. We realized that Stacie wanted to attend the middle school with her friends. This was the first real battle that I encountered with my daughter. I discovered that she had a rebellious streak in her personality. In elementary school Stacie pretty much got everything she wanted. I really spoiled her to the extreme, but now was the time for me to exert my fatherly prerogative and rebuke her choice to attend the middle school where her friends were enrolling. I gave my daughter a stern lecture about making good decisions, especially decisions related to peer pressure, her academics and her future. I had to remind myself about the conversations I had with my daughter about expressing her convictions with me and her mom.

I told her that she could disagree with her parents about an issue as long as she was mature enough and respectful with her viewpoint. In turn I promised her that we would listen to her and consider her point of view before making a decision about her life. The bottom line in reaching a decision would rest on this question: "What would be the best course of action to take concerning Stacie's well-being and success for her future?". I explained to her that in some situations she might be able to convince her parents to say yes to her desires, but on the other hand, I told her that she might not understand some of the decisions we would make about her life. She would have to trust us with her life. We used this parenting approach for each decision we had to make about our daughter's life.

Stacie developed into a good negotiator when we were at odds about a particular issue. She would win her share of debates and we were comfortable with giving her room to prove that she could be a responsible young lady--so we allowed Stacie to attend the middle school of her choice.

The next hurdle was high school; again, Stacie qualified to attend one of the best high schools in the city; unfortunately, it was an all girls school and she wanted no parts of an all girls school. That's when I began to notice her interest in boys. I knew this day would come but, I was not ready to deal with it. I had a vision and a plan for my daughter's life that did not include dating as a fifteen year old freshman in high school. But as the saying goes, the best laid plans of mice and men go awry. Stacie negotiated her way into attending Paul Lawrence Dunbar High School Health for Professions. Her desire was to become a registered nurse, but she met a young man at Dunbar and fell into "puppy love". Her plans took a sudden detour. She became pregnant at the tender age of sixteen. I went ballistic, but I remember the exact words my daughter said to me on the day I discovered that she was pregnant. "Daddy, I am still going to complete my plan to graduate from high school, graduate from college and become a registered nurse; my plan will be accomplished, but in a different way".

That was the day I realized that my daughter was one of the most mature and courageous sixteen year old young ladies on the planet. She did exactly what she said she would do. She also married her baby daddy, Rodrick James Harrison Sr. and together they are raising two wonderful children, Rodrick James Harrison Jr. and Ryann Gabrielle Harrison. Rodrick Sr. has developed and matured to become a good husband, father, and son-law. Rodrick Sr. received an Athletic/Academic Scholarship from the University of Maryland Baltimore County and he graduated with a B.S. degree in Information Systems. Rodrick Sr. also organized a prep basketball program in Baltimore with the assistance of co-organizer Brian Scott and coaching assistant Rodney "Noodles" Elliott. Rodney was a two-sport stand-out Scholar Athlete at Dunbar and he matriculated to the University of Maryland College Park on a full Athletic Scholarship. Rodney also received "3rd team All ACC basketball honors in his senior year at the school (1998).

Stacie and Leslee Scott also had significant input in the team's organizational structure. The Mt. Zion Warriors is comprised of a plethora of local, regional, and international basketball talent. Many of them have gone on to excel at some of the top Colleges and Universities Basketball Programs in the country. Kudos to Rodrick Sr. and company—keep up the good work guys!

Stacie graduated from Coppin State University with a B.S. degree in Nursing. She works as a Nurse Home Care Provider and she administers graceful care to all her patients.

Stacie is also my personal on-call nurse. She gives me a check-up from the feet up, from the neck up, and from the head up. Nurse Stacie scrutinizes my health habits with a laser focus. She does this when she visits me at home and when I speak with her on the phone. She usually says to me, dad did you do this or the other, and sometimes I respond—I did, or I plead the Fifth Amendment. I am hippopotamus glad and hallelujah happy about my Stacie, A.K.A. my chocolate brown baby girl. Stacie triumphed over the odds, just like her father did and now she is inducted into my "Against All Odds" Hall of Victory!

Now let me switch gears and turn your attention to the other gift from heaven; my son, Stephen M. Colbert Jr. He is an answered prayer. He was born on April 29, 1985. Before Stacie was conceived I prayed for a child. I did not ask the Lord for a female or a male child. I just wanted to be a father. After the birth of Stacie, I just thought it was the right thing to ask God for a male child. I believe most fathers can feel me on that. I even remember one day in 1984 when I was walking into a McDonalds Restaurant, I was compelled to stop and pray. I believe the Holy Spirit spoke to me and revealed to me that my prayer for a male child was answered. I got my meal from McDonalds, went home and said to my wife "I prayed for a son today and the Lord said yes". My wife said, "Ain't nothing coming out of this womb unless you put a ring on my finger.

I had been comfortable and content for a long time with having a baby momma, but on that day I came to my senses and realized that I had to grow up fast. God gave me an answer to my prayer and I realized that God answered Eva's prayer for a husband and a real father for our children. In 1984 we planned our wedding date for August 15, 1985. We also planned to conceive a baby boy. Stacie was born on August 15, 1978. We thought it would be a good thing to get married on our daughter's birthday. Stephen Jr. was born on April 29, 1985, about four months before Eva and me were married. All I can say is that God's ways are not our ways. He works by providence, not coincidence.

Stephen Jr. did not give us any drama for his first sixteen years on the planet. I am not exaggerating. Our son progressed through childhood and adolescence with seemingly no real problems. He was an unusually good kid.

He was smart, articulate, athletic, funny and lovable. He excelled in baseball at the Northwood Little League. He was a good basketball player, but he shied away from football. I supported him in his sports endeavors, but otherwise I pretty much left him alone to do his thing. I don't mean that in a negative way. Usually it is the problems and conflicts in life that make or break the relationship between father and son. But I was blind sided by the apparent absence of typical boy issues with my son; consequently, I neglected to spend quality time with Stephen Jr. like I did with my daughter.

Stephen entered Polytechnic High School as a freshman and that's when his interest in girls began to perk. He dated several girls during his tenure at Poly, but he did not appear to be serious about a long-term relationship with any of them. However, there was the girl across the street. I would have never imagined that Stephen would be engaged in an intimate relationship with this particular young lady, but it happened. It was not love at first sight, it was a young boy being guided by his testosterone and his hormones. A popular candy commercial best characterizes Stephen's experience with this particular young lady; the add read like this: "How many licks does it take to get to the center of a chewy tootsie-roll pop?"-- Stephen learned the answer. His playmate girl friend from across the street became pregnant and my son became a baby daddy. We were shocked by the news that our son had fathered a child at the tender age of 17. Believe me, he was not ready to raise a child. Stephen and the Baby's mother never developed a real relationship and there was no evidence to suggest that Stephen, his son, or his son's mother, would ever become a family. Stephen has always supported his son financially. But only time will tell if he gets the opportunity to raise his son (Jameir) in light of the current circumstances.

At the age of 22 Stephen's second child was born, a daughter by way of a different young lady friend. He is currently sharing parenting responsibilities with his baby's mother. He is striving to raise his daughter within this co-parenting relationship. So far Stephen and Skyler's Mom have formed a supportive environment for Skyler to grow and thrive. Stephen is learning to be a good father to his daughter. We have hope that in the coming years, he will be able to form a healthy co-parenting relationship with Jamier's Mom. My son has overcome some great challenges as a young adult father. He knows what his responsibilities are for raising his children and he is rapidly maturing as a father figure. To God be the Glory for turning around what could have been a family tragedy into a triumphant story.

Chapter 7

CAN ANYTHING GOOD COME FROM THE HOOD?

I believe if you interviewed one hundred Caucasian Suburbanites who were born and raised in middle class families, ninety percent would answer no to the question posed in the chapter heading. Their perception of life in black urban communities (i.e.; the hood) is tainted and prejudiced by stereotypical media reports and their own learned racism against black people whom they oppress without any provocation or logical reasoning. If you were to propose this same question to one hundred black people who live in the hood or who have been elevated from the hood to a suburban, middle class lifestyle, I believe ninety percent of the respondents would answer a resounding Yes!

This writer considers himself exhibit "A" among a long list of black people who have picked themselves up by their own boot straps, defied the odds, rose up and out of the ash heap of crime, violence and poverty to ascend to that deluxe apartment in the sky. I know many black people (family, friends, and acquaintances) who have persevered and triumphed over the negative predictions and fatalistic forecasts of some oppressive and racist white Americans. However, I must admit that I had the experience of meeting several Caucasian people who did not have a racist bone in their bodies. They were great human beings who cared about other human beings regardless of how white supremacists thought about them.

I consider myself to be a blessed and highly favored individual. One of my elementary teachers once said to me, "it's not the conditions you were born in that matters the most in life, but it is what you have been predestined to become that matters the most". I was born in what sociologist would consider to be an impoverished environment. But honestly, I did not know I was poor until the government told me so. I was identified by research studies and the federal census bureau as a victim of poverty. I was fed sufficiently, clothed, had shelter, health care, recreation, education, religion, a relatively safe neighborhood in the inner city, and most importantly a single parent who loved me and my siblings. My mother cared for us, cherished us, nurtured us and disciplined us to life. I was one happy kid living in poverty.

I believe that real poverty is found in the lives of the rich and famous. Poverty of mind and soul. When I was growing up you rarely heard about someone committing suicide, child abuse, rape, murder, etc. in the hood. The media refused to reveal the real deal in the dominant culture. There was also some sick and perverted stuff going on in affluent white communities as well as so called white trash and Hill-Billy Appalachian Communities. Everything from suicide to family incest. But the media projected and reflected these atrocities on black folk to keep the spotlight from shining on the mess of the so-called superior race. Black folk were used as scape goats for all the wickedness white folk did to themselves. If something was wrong in society black people were identified as the cause. But despite all of the oppressive forces at work in the minds and deeds of some white people, black people proved time and time again, generation after generation, that we are the most resilient and forgiving human on God's green earth. If white folk were the only group of people on earth, they would have self-destructed long ago. If they did not have black folk to blame, they would turn on each other and create a new species of "white negroes" in order to have someone to oppress and feel superior to.

But I am so glad that regardless of what the dominant culture believes about black lives; black lives matter, and white folk need to realize that they need us to survive. Don't get it twisted, black people are incredibly important to the survival of this nation and the planet. So yes, a lot of good people and good things have come from the hood. Let me share some good from the hood.

I was fortunate and blessed to grow up with some friends who I affectionately refer to as my "home boys or my dogs." I will introduce them by using a sports analogy. In the game of baseball there are nine players or positions. It just so happens that I know nine guys who I have played significant roles in my life. These guys have their own story of overcoming the odds in life. Their journeys intersected and paralleled with my journey in unique and providential ways. I believe God puts certain people in one's life on purpose and keeps others out on purpose so that one's purpose on earth can be accomplished according to his divine plan.

My lead-off hitter is a guy named Roger Dickens. I met Roger at The Community College of Baltimore in 1973. We were team mates on the Red Devils Junior College Basketball team. Roger A.K.A. "Roger the Dodger" had a unique handle while dribbling a basketball. He was able to dribble at a snail's pace and still manage to dazzle his defenders with a crazy crossover move that even Stephen Curry (NBA Star of the Golden State Warriors) would envy. He would leave his defenders spellbound as he dribbled by them on the way to scoring on an acrobatic lay up or a head twisting no look pass for an assist. Roger went on to star at Towson State University and was picked in the NBA draft by the Baltimore Bullets (renamed Washington Wizards). Roger rose from obscurity to stardom against all odds. He was cut from his high school basketball team at The Baltimore City College High School because the coach said he was too slow to compete against the leapers and dunkers on a star-studded team. Roger did not allow the coach's assessment of his skills deter him and the rest is history. Roger works as a recruiter in the office of Admissions at what is now the Baltimore Community College.

Next up is a fellow who became and still is my best friend. Fred Boh-Pete Wright. Fred was a star basketball player for Northern High School in Baltimore. He was an "East Baltimore Boy." He grew up idolizing players like Dickey Kelly and Skip Wise. Fred was an under rated player who always gave one hundred ten percent on the basketball court. I played against Fred while attending Douglass High School. Fred and I graduated in 1972. Fred was selected to the 2nd team All Maryland Scholastic Association (MSA). I was chosen for the 3rd team All-MSA squad. We were both recruited by Coach Jerry Phipps to play basketball at The Baltimore City Community College. We had to compete against each other for playing time at the small forward position. Coach Phipps did not play favorites, if one player got more time in the game than another player, it was because he earned the time in practice. Fred was always trying to run as fast as he could on the fast break because he knew that the first man down the court would be the recipient of an assist from Roger the Dodger.

I had the same mind set when I was in the game. Me and Fred competed vigorously to be the first man down court and score. We knew this was the best opportunity we had to put points in the books because the odds were against us being the first, second, or third option in an offensive scheme were our good buddy Tony Carter was the first option ninety percent of the time. Fred was recruited with me to play basketball for the Bowie State College Bulldogs in 1974. Fred and me transferred to Coppin State College and we played our senior year at the school in 1976. Coach John Banks and assistant coach Charlie "Grass Hopper" Moore welcomed us to the basketball team with open arms.

But more importantly, we had the opportunity to re-connect with Tony Carter and Eric King. We had played on teams together for many years prior to coming together at Coppin.

Fred left Baltimore after the Coppin experience and relocated in Omaha Nebraska. Fred completed his requirements for his B.S. degree and was appointed Vice-President of the Omaha, Nebraska Urban League in Lorraine County. Later, he was appointed CEO of the same organization. Fred was recruited to fill the position of Urban League President in Akron, Ohio. Fred currently works as a consultant for the University of Akron and he resides in Akron with his wife Judy. He is the proud father of three daughters; Channel, Annie, and Brandi, two grand-daughters, Torri and Tatum, and one grandson, Miles. Fred definitely qualifies as an odds beater. The account of his journey highlighted in this book is only the tip of the iceberg. Fred is a survivor and a thriver. Thank you Fred Wright, for being a part of my journey.

The third man up is none other than Tony "Put It Up" Carter. This guy was the first option on every basketball team he played on from school yard to college. I also played against Tony while attending Douglass High School in 1972. Tony was the best flat-footed shooter in Baltimore City high school basketball. The only elevation he seemed to have on his jump shot was when he stopped on a dime and raised his heels up and rested on his tip toes and released a line drive shot with the precision of a speeding bullet into the basket for two points. Tony also joined Roger, Fred, and me on the Baltimore Community College basketball team. He later starred at Coppin State College and helped the Eagles to win the National Athletic Interscholastic Association (N.A.I.A.) Basketball Championship in 1975. Tony went on to try out for the San Francisco Warriors of the NBA (Now the Golden State Warriors) and he also played professional basketball in South America for several years.

Their was another side to Tony's life that many respected and some feared. Tony was raised in Cherry Hill, a community located in Southwest Baltimore with a nearly one-hundred percent black population. Cherry Hill had a reputation for being a bad place where gangs and crime was the order of the day. But there were a lot of good hard working families in Cherry Hill. Tony used his basketball skills and his never give up attitude to emerge from Cherry Hill and shine a good light on his community.

Tony brought his rough and tough demeanor to the Community College of Baltimore in 1972. Tony had a way of motivating his team mates to put forth their best effort on the basketball court: "inspiration by intimidation". Tony would lay on the criticism loud and clear when one of his team mates made a mistake on the court. He hated to lose and hated players who played like wimps. Tony never backed down from a fight on or off the court. He was relentless in his pursuit of winning every time he stepped on the basketball court. Tony's motto was--you are either with me or against me. Despite his bully approach to leadership, Tony was well respected by his team mates and he motivated us to stand up for what we believed in. He was misunderstood by some but admired and revered by many dudes in the hood. Tony is now retired from the Walter C. Carter Center for Juveniles.

The number four man in the hood line up is Eric "Short Stop" King. Affectionately called short stop because he was 5 feet and 8 inches in height, but he refused to be intimidated by taller players on the court. He was short but his lack of height did not stop him from being one of the most tenacious and courageous basketball players I have ever known. His tenacity and courage extended beyond the basketball court. Eric was a fighter in life. He was a friend that I could trust to guard my back. Eric overcame the odds of growing up in the Edmondson Village area of West Baltimore. He attended Edmondson High School and went on to play basketball at Baltimore Community College. We never played against each other in high school. He was little Older than me, but our paths did cross at Coppin State College in 1976. Eric arrived at Coppin in 1975 and he burst onto the basketball scene seemingly out of nowhere. Tony Carter referred Eric to Coach John Bates and the rest is history. Eric helped lead the Coppin State basketball program to the 1975 N.A.I.A. National Division III Championship. Eric also set his eyes on graduating from Coppin and he transitioned to a career in the Baltimore County Public School System. I'm proud to report that he accomplished his goal. Eric and me where study buddies at Coppin. Every time I headed for the Library, Eric was right there with me. We collaborated on class projects and studied for exams together on a regular basis. We would carry our textbooks and assignments on road trips with us.

We played in games together and studied in dorm rooms and hotel rooms after away games. This impressed other team mates to join us in the mobile Study Hall. Eric is an overcomer and an example for anyone who struggles against the odds. Eric graduated from Coppin with a B.S. Degree and a M.ED. in Special Education. He also furthered his studies at Goucher College, where he earned a graduate certification in School Administration. Eric starred on the basketball court and in the classroom, and his son Eric Jr. excelled in football and academics at the McDonough School in Baltimore. Eric Jr. achieved a football scholarship from Wake Forest University in North Carolina, he graduated and he was drafted by the NFL Buffalo Bills. He played professional football for the Bills for one year. He played three years with the Tennessee Titans and two years each with the Cleveland Browns and the Detroit Lions. Eric Jr. now resides on the West Coast. This author and Eric Sr. still manage to hang out together with the other boys in the hood on occasions.

We will always maintain a strong bond as friends who overcame the odds and thrived in life. Eric Sr. also played professional basketball in South America for several years. Not bad for an ordinary guy who came from the hood in West Baltimore. Eric Sr. possessed an extraordinary amount of heart and courage. He lived in the hood, but he survived and thrived in life with an incredible success story. Eric Sr. passed a great legacy to his son and Eric Jr. took it to the next level.

Eric Sr. is currently employed by the Baltimore County School System as a Special Education teacher at Woodlawn High School. He has also held the position of Principal of an Evening School Alternative Program in Baltimore County. Major kudos to my friend Eric King Sr., a man's man and an odds beater.

Now I turn your attention to the non-athletic portion of the line-up. The fifth man up is Thelbert Ray Dawson, affectionately known as "Ray-Ray" or "Fats". I met Ray by chance at a homecoming football game between my school the Douglass Ducks and Ray's school, the Carver Vocational-Technical Bears. Ray stood out in that game because of his show boat and braggadocio personality. He was not one of Carver's key players, but no one would think that he was just a bench player because of all the claims he made about his football prowess when he entered the game. I took notice of Ray's arrogance during the game and it motivated me and my Mighty Ducks to bring a halt to Ray's showmanship at their homecoming game. We beat the bears soundly that day in October 1972 and Later when I officially met Ray at the Baltimore Community College in the fall of 1973, I never ceased to remind him of the 52 to 14 shellacking that my Ducks football team served to his Carver Bears.

I taunted Ray perpetually with the memory of what I called the massacre at Carver's Homecoming. Ray joined the football team at BCC and he continued to showboat on and off the field. His performance on the BCC football team seemed to be a repeat of his performance at Carver. He rarely got in games and he used his comedic talents to deflect from his bench riding role on the team. I vividly remember the BCC Homecoming game played in 1973 against a team from North Carolina. The score was 81 to 7 with about 3 minutes left in the game. Ray was called from the bench into the game for the first time.

His uniform was pure white, as clean as the board of health. Ray entered the game and did not make contact with an opposing player for the entire time he occupied the right defensive guard position that he played. We (Fred, Tony and me) laughed so hard that tears were streaming out of our eyes.

To add insult to injury, one of Ray's team mates suggested that he smear dirt on his uniform to show the fans that he had at least made contact with the football field during the game. We joked about this every chance we got while we were attending BCC. Despite Ray's clown show performance, he refused to concede that he was a misfit athlete. He tried playing basketball and was relatively good at the sport in light of his non-athletic physique. Again, Ray was the object of jokes and ridicule for his attempt to compete in the sport of basketball. But Ray never quit. He took the jokes like a man and whenever he was able to score a basket during a pick- up game he behaved like he had just won the pick-up basketball championship of the world. Although Ray did not have real success as an athlete, he was in his own world with the ladies. He gloated in his ability to carrel a stable full of plus sized women and he bragged about his sexual exploits to the guys every chance he got. We let Ray have his five minutes of fame when he talked about his latest catch. Ray was a mediocre athlete at best, but he was the "Barry White" for any plus sized girl who was open to be wined and dined by the fat man. A local D.J. Put it this way, "Nobody loves a fat man, but oh how a fat man can love". Still another radio personality contended that "it's not the size of the ship in the ocean, it's the motion". I will always remember my friend fats. He finished strong and refused to let other people define him. He lived his life on the wild side, but I witnessed the transformation of his life before he passed from earth to glory. Ray accepted Jesus Christ as his savior and he was called to preach the Gospel. His life turned at an 180 degree angle. He turned right and walked straight after overcoming the things that sought to destroy him. To God be the Glory for the great things he did through the yielded and transformed life of my buddy "Fats".

In the sixth spot in the line-up is a brother named Isaac Dickey McCauley. He was by far the most colorful and theatrical person I had ever met. He was a clown, a comedian and a showman all rapped up in one personality. I met Dickey at Coppin State College in 1975. Dickey was the Public-Address Announcer for the starting basketball line-up. He announced the five starting players at each home game similar to how Professional Boxing Announcer Vince McMann called out the names of opponents in the boxing ring. Dickey would create nick names for the starting five as well as the players who entered the game from the bench.

For example, when announcing Tony Carter he would use his baritone voice to say, "starting at the guard position, Tony Put It Up Carter"—referring to Tony's propensity to shoot the basketball more than any other player. Tony was given the green light by Coach John Bates and he made a high percentage of the shots he took. Dickey did the same type of announcement for each player on the team. He brought a high level of charisma to the games at Coppin and the fans who attended the basketball games came anticipating the showmanship that Dickey brought to the game of basketball at Coppin State College. Dickey was more than a basketball announcer to me.

He was my role model for academic achievement. He was the first one in our clan to earn a Bachelor's and a Master's degree at Coppin.

Dickey inspired me to think beyond basketball to my future. He often reminded me that my chances of earning a living as a basketball player was zero to none. I took his advice and started to assert myself academically and followed his footsteps to achieve a Bachelor's and a Master's degree from Coppin. Dickey even had great influence on my spiritual convictions. He survived the ravages of drug and alcohol addiction and surrendered his life to the Lord. Isaac became a Baptist Preacher. He enrolled in Seminary and devoted his life to ministry in the hood. I was inspired by his transformational life-style. I followed Isaac's example and became a Baptist Preacher, I enrolled in Seminary, and I also dedicated my life to inner city ministry.

Dickey and me supported each other in many ministry activities through the years. I was devastated when I received the news that he had passed away prematurely due to prostrate cancer. I recall him telling me that no one ever informed him about the history of prostrate cancer among the generations of men in his family. He said to me "if only I had been informed, I would have sought screening early on in my life". Later I too was diagnosed with an enlarged prostrate, but by the grace of God I have been able to manage the disorder through medical intervention. I will always cherish my relationship with my man Dickey, he was my road dog and an overcomer.

The seventh player on my hood team line up is also the oldest. I met this wise man through my sister Joanna and at the time he was serving as the pastor of the Church of God in Edmondson Village in Baltimore. I had been doing ministry for several years before I was introduced to "Elder Jake Butler". He took me under his wing, mentored me and gave me many opportunities to preach at his church and do outreach ministry in correctional facilities and street ministry. Even though I was getting excellent mentoring from my pastor at the New Psalmist Baptist Church (Bishop Walter S. Thomas). Elder Butler was a valuable part of my ministry development. After hearing my personal testimony about surviving many life-threatening ordeals, Elder Jake asked me to share my story with his congregation. He said his people needed to hear from a person who was delivered from drug addiction and other vices because most of his members had been raised in the church. They did not have any personal experience with the dark side of street life. They had issues like all human beings have, but not the close encounters with death and destruction that I survived. I gave the people at the Church of God the raw and transparent version of my life before I fell in love with Jesus. They seemed to be in awe and amazement each time I was given the opportunity to share my story with them. They requested me to come back and teach/preach at the church over thirty-five times during the course of my association with the church. The Church of God was truly my second home. They even considered me for the position of assistant to the Pastor. I was honored and humbled at the offer, but I was engaged heavily in prison ministry and inner-city outreach ministry at the time. I did not sense that the Lord was calling me away from my passion for the unchurched population to serve full time in the Church. I believed my calling was to the church without walls: the least, the last and the lost in the world. I continued to participate in ministry at the Church of God for many years, until the Lord gave me a vision to organize the City of Hope Church. Elder Butler, along with my Pastor, was instrumental in helping to guide me through the process of planting a new church. I am totally convinced that God did not lead me to take a position at the Church of God because it was his will for me to remain in the work he had called me to do. I absolutely believe that I was predestined to establish a church in the wilderness of the hood, to preach the good news to the poor. Elder Butler has transitioned from labor to rest and reward in glory land. His wisdom, his character, and his legacy still mentor me today.

The number eight batter in my line up is brother Roger Shaw. I met Roger at the Harlem Park Middle School in 1989. I was in my third teaching assignment in ten years and Roger was beginning his first year at the school. He had previously taught in the Dallas, Texas Public School System. Roger was a young enthusiastic black male teacher who demonstrated a strong passion for empowering black inner city-children who were caught in the net of poverty, labeling and miseducation. Roger and another super passionate black male teacher by the name of Dr. Andre Bundley, worked tirelessly to promote and implement an agenda to teach and mentor inner city children who being were left behind and abandoned by an ill-equipped school system and impoverished home environments. Dr. Bundley went on to lead the transformation of two schools in Baltimore. He also ran a very competitive race for Mayor of Baltimore City. Dr. Dr. Bundley is a powerful example of the good that came from the hood.

The majority of our students at Harlem Park Middle School were black, white, or Hispanic. They qualified for the free and reduced lunch program and most of them lived in single parent households. To add insult to injury, almost all of the students lived in high crime communities. Nevertheless, the staff at Harlem Park linked arms and hearts together to produce one of safest and most productive school cultures in the school system. Many of the teachers at Harlem Park ascended to high level administrative positions in the school system. Harlem Park became a model school for other middle schools that strived to elevate underachieving and impoverished public school students to perform consistent with other students in resource rich high performing school districts. Roger took the success he experienced at Harlem Park to the Paul Lawrence Dunbar

High School. He was appointed principal of the legendary East Baltimore School in 2001.

The School System CEO charged Roger with the task of reinvigorating a failing school in the midst of a contingent of prestigious alumni, community, and political leaders who yearned to see the academic resurgence of Dunbar High School. Principal Shaw was the Messiah they were waiting for. During his tenure he led the school to become one of the premier high schools in America. For so long Dunbar was known as one of greatest high school basketball programs in America, and now the football program was emerging as one of the best in the state of Maryland. But under Principal Shaw's leadership the "New Paul Lawrence Dunbar High School for Health Professions" emerged as the new kid on the block, receiving recognition from News Week Magazine and U.S. World Report, as one the top performing schools in America.

At last, Dunbar academics was being quoted in the same conversation as the basketball program. I was fortunate to join Roger at Dunbar in 2003 as an assistant principal. I was excited about the opportunity to jump on a train that was moving fast down the track of educational excellence. Using the work we engaged in at Harlem Park as a blueprint; Roger, myself, and other staff were able to transform Dunbar into a premier City-wide public high school with two Mantras: "Failure Is Not An Option" and "It Can Be Done".

Roger was promoted to the position of High School Director In 2007. This was a significant honor for Roger and the Dunbar family, however; the school and its constituents were in a happy-sad posture when Roger departed to assume his new role at Central Office. Roger had been the most charismatic and forward-thinking administrator in Dunbar's history; that being said, Roger left the school, but his spirit and leadership style continued to influenced the school program from a distance. Roger pulled some strings among the Central Office Hierarchy and he convinced the powers that be to appoint me to the position of managing assistant principal.

I was later appointed principal at Dunbar in 2008 and served in that capacity until my retirement in 2011. During our tenure at Dunbar teachers and students would inadvertently call me Mr. Shaw because me and Roger looked so much like each other physically as well as by-way of character traits and leadership style.

I was humbled and appreciative of being mistaken for the man who initiated the transformation of Dunbar High School. I close this narrative my recounting a great experience I shared with Roger, I would be remiss if I did not mention the revelation I received as we encountered students and families in crisis on a day to day basis. We agreed that we would refer to Dunbar as "The City of Hope" because of the way in which we handled seemingly hopeless situations that surfaced in the lives of students and parents at Dunbar. We had students who excelled academically but some of them looked like a train wreck in the making. We helped students and parents who found themselves hanging from the cliff of emotional disaster to find hope and persevere against all odds.

Roger Shaw helped to accomplish something great at Dunbar and I was invited to partner with him. I established a new church in 2007. We used the Dunbar auditorium as our place of worship on Sundays. The experience at Dunbar inspired me to name the church "The City of Hope Church". I don't think I have to explain the etymology of the name. To this day Roger and me still communicate and fellowship sharing awesome stories about the City of Hope! Roger currently works as the Director of the Baltimore City Public Schools Executive Director of Alternative Schools/Re-engagement Center.

Last, but not least, I want to talk about a man whom I have known all my life. I'm not taking about my father (never saw him a day in my life). I'm not talking about a brother, a mentor, or a friend. I speak of none other than my uncle; Bernard Jake Colbert Jr. also known in past times by the nick name, "Jake the Snake". He is now a new man in Christ.

He is a member of the Bethel A.M.E. Episcopal Church in Baltimore Maryland. Jake has overcome his own version of life threatening odds on his way to becoming a transformed man on a mission.

Jake opened up his heart to me about his life in the streets of Baltimore. So much so that I consider him to be an example of a miracle man. He shared with me his experience as a heroin dealer and user which led to a drug addiction that held him captive for many years. Jake reminded me of the character "Priest" in the 1972 movie "Superfly" (starring Ron O'Neal).

Jake was a flamboyant dresser and lady's man. He managed to stay employed at a local factory during his tenure as a street level drug dealer. I was completely baffled when I found out that he was entangled in this undercover drug dealer and drug user lifestyle. Maybe it was because I would later live the same kind of life style as a young adult. I did not realize that I was unknowingly living in the shadow of my uncle Jake. The two of us were at one point in our lives living simultaneously on the same path to destruction. There was a period of time when we got high together and we schemed together and we were co-signing on one another's misery. But thanks be to God that that we both reached a turning point in our lives and received Jesus Christ as our Savior and Lord. I believe our conversion experiences happened within a year apart.

Jake told me that he had received Jesus into his life in a jail cell. He was arrested for a number of different crimes and he was placed in a cell with inmate who was smuggling heroin into the jail. Jake revealed to me that one night his cell mate was cooking up some heroin in the cell and the smell of the dope came drifting up to his bunk. He inhaled the fumes and immediately realized that even in jail he could not escape the presence and menace of heroin. He prayed and asked the Lord for a miracle in the cell. He was sick and tired of being sick and tired of watching his life dissolve right before his eyes. It was as if Jake was cooking his life in a spoon, just like he had done so many times with the white poison called heroin or smack.

The cell mate offered Jake a hit, and for the first time in his life, Jake was able to resist and conquered the monkey on his back. Jake had experienced God's deliverance power for the first time in his life. He had to suffer through painful withdrawal symptoms, but it would not be in vain. Jake's cell mate was soon miraculously moved to another cell in the jail and Jake was able to serve the remainder of his jail time in a drug free cell. He said the experience was better than a drug detox program or a drug recovery program. The Lord kept Jake in the cell clean and drug free. When he was released he hit the ground running straight to the Church.

Jake's Pastor asked him to become a member of the Church substance abuse ministry and again, he hit the ground running. The Bible instructs believers to "Be very careful, then, how you live-not as unwise but as wise, making the most of every opportunity, because the days are evil" (Ephesians 5:16 NIV). Jake has applied the word of God to his life and his faith has been richly rewarded.

Jake had a greater vision that led him to organize the New Life Supportive Housing Program in Baltimore Md. He has written grants and received government funding to provide drug counseling and employment training for recovering addicts, ex-offenders and homeless men.

To God be the Glory for the transforming work he has performed in the lives of the nine men I met in the hood. They represent my "All Hood" All Star Team.

Chapter 8

THE CITY OF HOPE

I have heard and read many definitions of hope in my lifetime but the one I was most inspired by is the definition from the Revell Bible Dictionary. The author defines hope as an eager and confident expectation that sustains a person while he or she is waiting patiently for fulfillment. I am absolutely convinced that without hope, no person can survive the vicissitudes of life. Anyone who lives without hope is like a person stuck in quick sand with nobody around to hear their frantic and desperate cry for help. It's only a matter of time before the person is sucked and pulled down to the bottom of the quick sand pit. I know people who have died Prematurely because of hopelessness. Hopelessness can be reversed if an individual is able to look up for a mere second and encounter the God of hope. No matter how long a person has been suffering, God is always one prayer away. Regardless of one's condition or predicament, the light of God can shine in the darkest place and slip through the smallest crack in a broken life. Hope in God is the antidote for all that ails humanity. Faith and prayer are vital tools in the toolbox of one's life, but hope is the real game changer.

Faith can move a person forward and out of darkness one step at a time and it will sometimes push a person ahead by leaps and bounds. Prayer will allow a person to have a two-way conversation with God; asking and believing God for healing and deliverance.

But faith and prayer usually require a period of waiting. Oh yes, God can bring about healing miraculously and instantly, but that does not seem to be the norm for the dispensation that we are living in today.

Don't be fooled by the sensational theatrics produced by some Tele-Evangelistic Miracle Money Driven Programs. They are nothing more than organized, money grabbing programs. They are not authentic God directed and sanctioned ministries.

I know many people with good intentions who were duked and spun into a state of ecstasy after being hoodwinked by false crystal ball readers in clerical garb. I have learned that circumstances can't be prayed away or eliminated by mustering up enough faith. Even the greatest and most faithful heroes of the Christian faith still echo today in agreement that even with pure faith and prayer, one must learn to wait on the Lord. Wait on the Lord by faith; in prayer, but with hope. Wait on God's perfect timing. God always keeps his promises and he delivers on time every time.

I knew hopelessness for a season of my life, but now I have hope for the rest of my life. People **"who hope"** things will change really believe change is possible and even probable but not certain. People **"who have hope"** that things will change believe the promises of God will be fulfilled in their lives. They carry the promises of God like a football player carries the ball down field across the goal line. My breakthrough came when I changed my vocabulary. I stopped saying to myself, "I hope things change", rather I started declaring **"I have hope"** that things will change. I had the spirit of **"My Great Unbeatable God"** of the universe resident in my being.

65

Here is my personal illustration of how faith, prayer and hope helped me to survive and thrive against all the adversity in my life. Faith is the starter pistol in the race against the odds. Prayer is the conversation a track runner has with the Lord as he or she is running toward the finish line. The race may be 100-yard dash, a 440 relay race or a grueling marathon. Hope is the power to endure and not give up during the race.

The runner can't see the finish line from a distance but he or she knows that the finish line exists. Hope enables the runner to run with patience the race that is set before him or her. How does a runner run with patience?

How does a person who has become restless in the pursuit of healing find patience? Hope informs the runner that there is a God-set time to arrive at the finish line. When one runs with patience they run with the same vigor, vitality and velocity as an Olympic runner would run, but the person who has hope in God rests in the finished work of Christ on the Cross while running toward the finish line. In other words when a person runs a race with hope in God he or she is not concerned with finishing the race in a specific amount of time, rather the person is only focused on getting to the finish line at the time set by God. They run looking unto Jesus, the author and finisher of their faith.

Another illustration crossed my mind while I was ordering breakfast at a local McDonald's restaurant. I received my receipt from the cashier and walked to the "Pick Up Order Here" line to wait for my order. In about three minutes the server called my number and handed me my order. I did not have to hope that I would receive my order. I could see the cook preparing the order. But hope in God requires the person who is waiting on a promise from God to wait eagerly with confidence without being able to see the cook.

One has to have hope in the invisible cook (God). The word of God says "While we look not at the things which are seen: but at the things which are not seen: for the things which are seen are temporal; but the things which are not seen are eternal (II Corinthians 4:18).

Like an appointment date to see a Physician. The date, time and place of the appointment is written in advance by the Doctor. For example, an appointment for April 17 is actually written on March 17. The patient waits in anticipation for an event that he or she will participate in thirty days in the future. As the patient looks at the calendar each day, he or she is also looking at the appointment date.

The patient moves closer to the appointment date confident that the appointment will be made, because the doctor has never failed to keep an appointment and deliver a positive report. The patient is eager to get to the Doctor's office. The written appointment becomes the substance of things hoped for and the evidence of things not seen yet. For thirty days the patient has hope that the promise of an appointment will be kept.

When the patient walks into the Doctor's office on March 17 hope becomes a reality. In other words, hope in God is a guarantee that the one who waits on the Lord will never be disappointed. A child of God is able take one day at a time regardless of the trouble each day might bring.

Have you ever said "I can't wait for a certain thing to happen", but you knew you that you would have to wait until it happened. You were actually moving forward with a laser focus towards your goal.

How do you wait on God and put your hope in him? Do you wait and hope like some people do in the dentist office for a tooth extraction. Some people dread the thought of sitting in the dentist office, let alone the dentist chair. Or do you wait like you wait for your next birthday. Your birthday may be months away so you enjoy other blessings and do other things while you wait for your birthday to come.

A few weeks before your birthday arrives, you began to eagerly anticipate your big day; in other words, you just can't wait for your big day.

But you know that you have to wait to participate in what you had anticipated for 365 days. You moved forward with patience toward the birthday that was set before you. I cherish these powerful illustrations of hope in God and I have hope that you will embrace them as you display hope in God in your life.

It was hope that steered me through the darkest days of my life, and it was hope that motivated me to embrace the vision from God to establish and organize the "City of Hope Church" in 2007.

The burden for people existing in hopelessness hijacked me and led me to go and help my people find the salvation and deliverance that I found in my hopeless state. I consulted with my Pastor (Bishop Walter S. Thomas Sr.), he gave me the green light and I ran with the vision God had given to me. Faith, Prayer, Grace, and Favor linked hands with hope and formed an unbreakable chain that has held the City of Hope Church together.

On November 12, 2017 we celebrated 10 years of ministry to the least, the last, and the lost in Baltimore City. We chose to use the following mantra to exemplify and magnify the character of the Church: The City of Hope Church-"Where Hope Is Contagious".

We believe that hope in God is indeed contagious because of the evidence of the changed lives in our church. God sent people who did not have hope to a Church with a message of hope to see and hear the life changing testimonies of ordinary people. Pastor Rick Warren writes in his book, The Purpose Driven Church, that the "greatest advertisement of a Church is changed lives". When people see other people who have been delivered from the same conditions that they are currently held hostage to, hope in God can become contagious.

A friend of mine once said to me that "Christianity is caught more than it is taught". People tend to gravitate to the light of ordinary people whom they can relate to.

Many different kinds of people have come through the door of the City of Hope Church during our ten year existence. Our congregation consists of persons with three primary profiles; transients, revolvers, and settlers. Some come and go, some come and leave only to return later, some come and have remained. Eighty percent of our members fall into one or more of the following categories: Unemployed or entry level jobs, poor literacy skills, recipients of some kind of social service assistance, generational poverty, drug and/or alcohol recovery programs, blended families, single parent families, ex-offenders and repeat offenders.

Twenty percent of our Church membership include persons with college degrees or credits, professional careers and families with strong support.

The twenty percent carry the financial weight of the Church, but they do it faithfully and lovingly. They believe God has called them to bear the infirmities of the weak. They know that to whom much is given, much is required.

There are no salaries provided to staff at the Church. The work of the Church is funded by the promises in the word of God. We ask, seek, and knock for resources. We believe and we trust the Lord to supply all of our need according to his riches in Glory by Christ Jesus. God is our financial planner, advisor and provider for life, health, and prosperity. Amen!

Sixty percent of the members at the City of Hope were evangelized and baptized as new converts to the Christian faith. The remainder of the members came with some level of Christian experience. This is The City of Hope Church, "Where Hope Is Contagious".

Chapter 9

WINNER BY UNANIMOUS DECISION

I will use a heavyweight boxing analogy to share how Hope in God transformed my life from apparent defeat to total victory. Allow me to use my imagination and become a fight announcer. I will introduce the opponents or challengers that tried to knock me out. The announcer belts out over the Public Address -- "in the corner to my left the **15** contenders; **A** near fatal car accident at the age of **8, A** Fever of **106** at the age of **10, A** near fatal knife wound at the age of **15, A** bullet that missed at age **16, A** drug and alcohol addiction at the age of **18, A** Suicide ideation at the age of **25, A** Diagnosis of Clinical Depression at the age of **32, A** Diagnosis of hypertension at the age of **40, A** Diagnosis of BPH (benign prostatic hyperplasia – i.e.; enlarged prostrate gland) at age **45, A** Diagnosis of Glaucoma at the age of **60, A** Diagnosis of Iatrogenic diabetes insipidus and type 2 diabetes mellitus at the age of **62. A** diagnosis of Rheumatoid Arthritis at the age of **62, A** diagnosis of Stage G3a/A1 Kidney disease at the age of **62,** and **A** diagnosis of Secondary Hyperparathyroidism at the age of **62**".

Now the ring announcer turns to the other corner and he speaks into the P.A. System and says, "Ladies and Gentlemen and boxing fans all over the world, I direct your attention to the corner to my right, to the fighter in the red trunks, weighing in at 175 pounds; the defending heavy weight champion of the world, Pastor Stephen *'Stick-Man'* Colbert: Now let's get ready to *R–U–M–B–L–E*!"

Fifteen fights against 15 different medical conditions. I was knocked down to the mat many times in each fight. The referee gave me the standing ten count several times in each fight. But I got back up from the mat each time. The bell sounded to end the round before the referee could finish the ten count and I was able to retreat and recover in my corner. I had the greatest fight manager in the world and he doubled as my corner cut man. Jesus Christ was my cut man, he was my healer, he was my comforter, he was my strength, he was my word, he was my wisdom and he was my encourager. I was able to bounce back and get back in the ring because Jesus gave me an unbreakable spirit. I liken my spirit to the bounce back action of one of my favorite childhood toys—"Weeble Wobble".

Weeble Wobble was a trade mark for children's roley-poley toys originating in Hasbro's play school collection in the 1970's.

Tipping an egg-shaped Weeble causes a weight located at the bottom-center to be lifted off the ground. Once released, gravitational force brings the Weeble back into an upright position. I fought my medical conditions like I was a Weeble Wobble man.

Jesus was the weight in the center of my life. This is what I say to encourage all the Weeble Wobble people in the world: "If anyone tells you that you will not recover from a tragedy in your life, look them straight in the eyes and respond with these declarations:

If you can peep at my disability, don't forget to stare at my ability.

If you can't understand my process, just watch my progress.

If you are confused by my reality, wait to see my actuality and my destiny; and my condition is not my conclusion!"

Fifteen fights with the unbeatable God on my side. Fifteen fights that I not only survived, but I won each one by unanimous decision.

Fifteen fights that I escaped from without a crippling or disabling condition.

Fifteen fights from age 8 to age 62, now I'm looking forward with hope and a future. I am a winner in life by unanimous decision!

I am ecstatically happy about the recent medical reports I received from my doctors (October 11, 2017).

Based the results of a battery of lab tests each one of the fifteen medical conditions cited in this book have been stabilized and managed or reversed. I will be forever grateful for the excellent care I received from all my doctors, nurses and other medical staff during and after my hospitalization.

WINNERS NEVER QUIT

I end this chapter with another amazing account of my life against all odds. On Monday October 23, 2017, I participated in a basketball game at the age of sixty-three years young. To add even more amazement to this event, the location of the basketball game was at the Francis Scott Key Middle School, located at 1425 E. Fort Ave. in Baltimore Md., I taught 8th grade math to special needs students at the school in 1985. One might call my return to the school a Deja vu experience, but I will call it a providential act of God. I was admitted to the hospital while teaching at the school in 1986. I totally collapsed emotionally under the pressure of life in it's mixed and various states. Even under the stress, I managed to receive superior evaluations from the former principal, Gene Lawrence.

Principal Lawrence noted in one of my yearly evaluations, that I was one of the best special education teachers he had ever observed in a classroom setting.

Now in 2017, 32 years later, I returned to the school to play basketball with a group of players in the Volo City Basketball league. The average age of the players was 31. The league is sponsored by the Volo City Kids Foundation (volocity.org.)

My son, Stephen Jr. jokingly recruited me to play in the game and he was surprised when I showed up in my basketball gear ready to play. The coach said "put this man into the game". He put me in and I played, and I felt incredibly awesome! On Monday October 23, 2017 at approximately 9:00 p.m., I found the favor of God at the place of one of my biggest setbacks—The Francis Scott key Middle School.

The first anniversary of my hospital admittance was November 25th, 2017. That's the day I was rushed to the Sinai hospital with a Blood Sugar Level of 1100. I survived and now I am thriving in good health and prosperity. I would like to declare November 25th as **"AGAINST ALL ODDS DAY"**!

Beloved, I bid you a good day, and a long healthy and prosperous life: "Now unto him that is able to keep you from falling, and present you faultless before his glory with exceeding great joy, to the only wise God our Savior, be glory and majesty, dominion and power, both now and ever, Amen. (Jude 1:24-25 KJV).

About the Author

Pastor Stephen Mallory Colbert Sr. is a proud native of Baltimore.

He is passionate about ministry to the lost, the least and the last members of society. Pastor Colbert received his formal education from the Frederick Douglas High School in Baltimore; the Community College of Baltimore (Recreational Leadership Major); Coppin State University (B.S. Degree in Special Education and a Master's Degree in Rehabilitation Counseling); the John's Hopkins University School of Professional Studies in Business and Education (Graduate Certificate in School Administration and Supervision); and the St. Mary's Seminary and University Ecumenical Institute (Theological Studies Program).

Pastor Colbert retired in June 2011 after 32 years of committed service to Baltimore's public school students, which included three wonderful years as the Principal of the renowned *"Paul Lawrence Dunbar High School"*.

Pastor Colbert serves as the pastor of the City of Hope Church. He also makes himself available to minister to people in the community, the prisons, drug recovery programs, mental health centers and mentoring programs.

Pastor Colbert currently volunteers part-time in the Baltimore City Public School System Re-Engagement Center where he assists with identifying and reinstating high school drop outs who desire to obtain their high school diplomas.

Pastor Colbert also works part-time in the BCPS Office of Achievement and Accountability where he is assigned to monitor the administration of district and state-wide testing programs.

Pastor Colbert and his lovely wife of 38 years, Eva, love to travel and vacation. He enjoys spending quality time with his two adult children (Stacie and Stephen Jr.) and his four grandchildren; Rodrick, Ryann, Jamier and Skyler.

Pastor Colbert's life is driven by two mantras: "My life is for Service and My Service is for Life" and "My aim in life is to wear-out helping others and enjoy life to the fullest". I plan to avoid sitting around the house rusting out in retirement. **Amen!!!**

Printed in the United States
By Bookmasters